Changing the Narrative
Information Campaigns,
Strategy and Crisis Escalation
in the Digital Age

Lawrence Freedman and Heather Williams

Changing the Narrative
Information Campaigns, Strategy and Crisis Escalation in the Digital Age

Lawrence Freedman and Heather Williams

IISS The International Institute for Strategic Studies

The International Institute for Strategic Studies

Arundel House | 6 Temple Place | London | WC2R 2PG | UK

First published September 2023 by **Routledge**
4 Park Square, Milton Park, Abingdon, Oxon, OX14 4RN

for **The International Institute for Strategic Studies**
Arundel House, 6 Temple Place, London, WC2R 2PG, UK
www.iiss.org

Simultaneously published in the USA and Canada by **Routledge**
52 Vanderbilt Avenue, New York, NY 10017

Routledge is an imprint of Taylor & Francis, an Informa Business

© 2023 The International Institute for Strategic Studies

DIRECTOR-GENERAL AND CHIEF EXECUTIVE Sir John Chipman KCMG
SERIES EDITOR Dr Benjamin Rhode
ASSISTANT EDITOR Michael Marsden
EDITORIAL Alice Aveson, Jill Lally, Gráinne Lucey-Tremblay, Adam Walters
PRODUCTION Alessandra Beluffi, Ravi Gopar, Jade Panganiban, James Parker, Kelly Verity
COVER PICTURE Stockbyte/Getty Images

The International Institute for Strategic Studies is an independent centre for research, information and debate on the problems of conflict, however caused, that have, or potentially have, an important military content. The Council and Staff of the Institute are international and its membership is drawn from almost 100 countries. The Institute is independent and it alone decides what activities to conduct. It owes no allegiance to any government, any group of governments or any political or other organisation. The IISS stresses rigorous research with a forward-looking policy orientation and places particular emphasis on bringing new perspectives to the strategic debate.

The Institute's publications are designed to meet the needs of a wider audience than its own membership and are available on subscription, by mail order and in good bookshops. Further details at www.iiss.org.

British Library Cataloguing in Publication Data
A catalogue record for this book is available from the British Library

Library of Congress Cataloging in Publication Data

ADELPHI series
ISSN 1944-5571

ADELPHI AP493–495
ISBN 978-1-032-70786-0

Contents

AUTHORS

Sir Lawrence Freedman is Emeritus Professor of War Studies at King's College London, where he was Professor of War Studies from 1982 to 2014 and Vice-Principal from 2003 to 2013. He was educated at Whitley Bay Grammar School and the universities of Manchester, York and Oxford. He previously held research appointments at the IISS, Nuffield College Oxford and Chatham House. Elected a Fellow of the British Academy in 1995, he was appointed Official Historian of the Falklands Campaign in 1997. In June 2009 he was appointed to serve as a member of the official inquiry into Britain's role in the 2003 Iraq War.

Heather Williams is the director of the Project on Nuclear Issues and a senior fellow in the International Security Program at the Center for Strategic and International Studies (CSIS). She is also an associate fellow with the Project on Managing the Atom in the Belfer Center for Science and International Affairs at Harvard Kennedy School. Until 2022 she was a senior lecturer in defence studies at King's College London. She has a PhD in war studies from King's College London, an MA in security-policy studies from the George Washington University, and a BA in international relations and Russian studies from Boston University.

ACKNOWLEDGEMENTS

We are grateful to the IISS, particularly Benjamin Rhode, for supporting this volume and for all their substantive suggestions and editorial inputs. The idea for this project began in early 2017, and the world has certainly changed since then, with narratives and social media playing an ever-increasing role. When we began the project, Donald Trump was still active on Twitter, Russia's second invasion of Ukraine was not yet a reality, and China was largely absent from the competition of narratives on the geopolitical stage. As a result, this manuscript has undergone many updates, and many individuals and organisations have supported its evolution.

Justin Anderson, Vipin Narang, Carl Robichaud and Scott Sagan were early supporters of this research and offered helpful insights throughout its development. For research assistance at various stages of the project we are grateful to Nicolas Adamopoulos, Alexi Drew, Jamie Kwong, Lachlan MacKenzie, Amelia Morgan, Joseph Rodgers and Reja Younis.

For institutional support we are grateful to the Department of War Studies and Centre for Science and Security Studies at King's College London, the Center for Strategic and International Studies, and the Project on Managing the Atom at Harvard Kennedy School, with particular thanks to Matthew Bunn, Francesca Giovannini and Steven Miller.

INTRODUCTION

This book assesses the impact of state-led information campaigns, largely conducted through social media, on crisis escalation and the international competition for strategic advantage. By 'information campaign' or 'information operation' we mean an attempt by an individual or a group – which could be a state – to establish, shape or challenge a narrative; this effort may encompass what could be described as 'propaganda', 'public diplomacy' or 'disinformation', or even 'fake news'. By a 'narrative' we mean a storyline that interprets events in a way that legitimises the narrator's behaviour and encourages others to act in a way that serves their purposes. There is nothing new about such activities, but this book seeks to explore their significance within a contemporary information environment that is heavily influenced by the internet and social-media platforms.[1]

Given the speed with which information can spread on social networks, the relatively low cost of its propagation, and the potential consequences of national narratives being shaped by these means, various analysts have identified these networks as highly significant factors in contemporary strategy and crisis management. We agree that digital information campaigns have potential strategic significance and deserve careful study, but having examined a number of information campaigns during recent international crises, we are also cautious in assessing the effects of such campaigns. They need to be located within their broader context. Whatever their instigators may intend, their actual effects can be hard to predict or control. Public perceptions turn out to be quite difficult to change and not easily shaped by information from unfamiliar sources. This is why information campaigns are often more effective with domestic audiences, to whom they are more naturally tailored, than with foreign ones. With some exceptions, narratives do not travel well. Influencing thinking in other countries usually depends on knowledge of pre-existing divisions that can be exploited. At times of crisis, social media can also be used to transmit messages between political leaders in an unusually direct and explicit form. Our analysis is concerned with the extent to which either these broader information campaigns or more elite-level messaging can affect crisis behaviour, including the potential for escalation.

The new information environment

Social-media platforms such as Twitter, Facebook, Instagram, WhatsApp, VKontakte and WeChat have become the media sources of choice for many users around the world, including leading political figures. Less than 20 years ago, these platforms seemed to be a revolutionary development; now they are accepted as one of the primary means by which individuals, organisations and governments engage with their discrete and wider communities. Although our focus is predominantly on Twitter, due to its status as the pre-eminent platform for official statements and news in Western countries, we also examine other platforms as their role and significance varies by country.

(We are aware that recent problems with Twitter have led to the development of alternative platforms performing a similar function, such as Bluesky and Threads. To add to the confusion, Twitter has been rebranded as 'X'.)

Marshall McLuhan famously observed that 'the medium is the message', referring to the way that forms of messaging affect social structures irrespective of content.[2] A post on Twitter (a tweet), for example, is shaped by its sudden appearance and its brevity – the first tweets were only 140 characters long, although this was later doubled to 280. Like other social networks, Twitter is a 'noisy' medium, so a particular message must compete for attention with a multitude of others being posted simultaneously. It is no simple task to cut through and gain notice. Every message is at risk of being crowded out as thousands more soon pile up behind it. The digital age is marked by a surfeit rather than a scarcity of information. Individuals can choose between a multitude of alternative sources of news and stories to consider, rather than making do with a few easily accessible sources. Without much effort it is possible to scan numerous sites for information, detecting material that would never have been found in earlier times. Much of this information appears in largely headline form, not requiring careful comprehension, with little or no sense of the reliability of the source. Because individuals can choose whom to follow on social media, they can pre-select their information, which often aligns with their pre-existing views. So, despite the mass of diverse material available, often the effect is most powerful in reinforcing existing attitudes.

The billions of messages posted worldwide each day support a variety of social and political functions, benign as much as malign. Many are about everyday matters such as holidays, films, investments and charitable giving, rather than political views and partisan commitments. Even messages on more contentious topics tend to be aimed less at changing views than at demonstrating affinity with those who already share those views. Attention has naturally focused on the darker side of social media, especially the ease with which provocative, inflammatory and defamatory material can be generated and spread. Such material is frequently personalised and directed at celebrities and politicians or used to target specific groups. Users can quickly and simply enter into another country's debates anonymously or under an assumed name without any requirement to be open or honest about their identity.

Social-media platforms are subject to the policies of their owners and government regulators. The ability of a few companies or even individuals to control how people engage with each other raises questions of unaccountable power. This also relates to companies' ability to learn about their users' lives and to exploit this information for targeted advertising, or to sell it to organisers of political campaigns. As a form of communication, social networks continue to evolve.[3] As instruments of international communication, they can facilitate frank negotiations of an arms-control agreement, while they can also be manipulated to stir up nationalism during a crisis.[4] Social media also plays a role in contemporary geopolitics and conflict: world leaders have used it to threaten military strikes, call for peace, open negotiations and appeal to their political bases.[5]

The Trump effect

The question of social media's role in advancing political narratives gained in salience through Donald Trump's use of Twitter. He was an early adopter of the platform when his political ambitions were nascent; he later made it his default mode of communication as a US presidential candidate and then as president. His example first raised concerns about how Twitter activity might lead to instability at home and abroad. His account was suspended in early 2021 because of his false allegations that the November 2020 presidential elections had been fraudulent and the perceived risk, in the aftermath of the attack on the Capitol on 6 January 2021, that his Twitter account could incite further violence.[6] The suspension was lifted after Elon Musk acquired Twitter and became its CEO in October 2022.

After he opened his Twitter account in 2009, Trump's early tweets were bland, but from 2011 onwards he began to use them to augment and adapt his brand as a combative, outspoken personality. Soon president Barack Obama became a major target as Trump moved further into the political sphere. By the time he began his campaign for the Republican presidential nomination in 2015, he had a mass following and understood more than rival candidates about how social media could be used for political advantage. Trump pioneered a Twitter-based demagoguery, exploiting the polarisation the format encouraged, and continued this into his presidency. His tweeting then became even more significant, not only because of the inherent status of his office but also because he could make his views known while bypassing the normal bureaucratic checks. Before his account was suspended on 8 January 2021, Trump sent 26,236 tweets as US president.[7] Irrespective of their appropriateness or literacy, most could be understood as authoritative presidential statements. Trump set an online path for others to follow, including Indian Prime Minister Narendra Modi and Ayatollah Ali Khamenei of Iran.

As head of state, Trump's tweets were distinctive because they were cast as informal interventions. In principle this was not significantly different from unscripted or poorly expressed remarks at a press conference. Yet Trump's tweets were more deliberate and could also exploit Twitter's special reach and immediacy. Their potential importance first became clear in the case of North Korea. On 2 January 2017, shortly before his inauguration, Trump issued his first Twitter warning to the hermit kingdom:

> North Korea just stated that it is in the final stages of developing a nuclear weapon capable of reaching parts of the U.S. It won't happen![8]

To Trump's frustration, this did not stop Kim Jong-un from testing nuclear weapons and missiles. In July 2017, when a North Korean missile landed close to Japan, Trump responded on Twitter:

> North Korea has just launched another missile. Does this guy have anything better to do with his life?[9]

As the situation deteriorated, with reports that North Korea could mount a small nuclear warhead on a missile, Trump responded not with a tweet but with remarks to journalists delivered from one of his golf courses: 'North Korea best not make any more threats to the United States. They will be met with fire and fury like the world has never seen.'[10] This was followed by a speech at the United Nations during which he described the North Korean leader as 'Little Rocket Man' – a term he had also used on Twitter – using a reference to an Elton John song that included a dig at Kim's height. Kim responded by promising to 'definitely tame the mentally deranged US dotard with fire'.[11]

Trump decided that Kim was a bully. Bob Woodward reports that he told an aide, 'He's a tough guy. The way to deal with those people is by being tough. And I'm going to intimidate him and I'm going to outfox him.'[12] After Kim's New Year's Day 2018 address, in which he expressed confidence that the United States was deterred because 'a nuclear button is always on the desk of my office', Trump retorted on Twitter:

North Korean leader Kim Jong Un just stated that the 'Nuclear Button is on his desk at all times.' Will someone from his depleted and food starved regime please inform him that I too have a Nuclear Button, but it is a much bigger & more powerful one than his, and my Button works![13]

The most dangerous moment came when Trump planned to tweet that he was ordering the departure from South Korea of all US military dependants – the thousands of family members of the 28,500 troops stationed there.[14] This was likely to be taken as a sign of imminent attack by the US armed forces. He was dissuaded from posting the tweet. Yet when in March 2018 the South Koreans conveyed an invitation from Kim to a summit, Trump accepted immediately. The leaders met in Singapore in June that year and gave the impression of cooperation and diplomatic progress, even to the point of denying there was an issue when it became clear that Kim had no interest in the 'denuclearisation' process that was supposed to be at the heart of the summit communiqué.

In Jeffrey Lewis's clever fictional novel *The 2020 Commission*, a report examines the reasons for a North Korean nuclear attack on the US in 2020, with a presidential tweet playing a crucial role in the story.[15] The novel depicts the brief rapprochement of 2018 followed by a deterioration in relations, marked by a series of hostile and mocking tweets from Trump as North Korea fails to denuclearise. A crisis arises when North Korean air defences shoot down a South Korean civilian airliner that has drifted off course, having mistaken it for a military plane. Without consulting Washington, South Korean president Moon Jae-in retaliates with a small number of conventional-missile strikes against North Korean targets. Kim misinterprets a tweet from Trump boasting that 'LITTLE ROCKET MAN WON'T BE

BOTHERING US MUCH LONGER' and mistakenly assumes an attempt to destroy the North Korean regime is under way. He responds with nuclear strikes against South Korea, Japan, and US bases in the region.

Fiction can often illuminate real strategic issues. In principle, this scenario demonstrates the power of social media in the wrong hands. But it also reminds us that the effect of such messages depends on context. In the story, Trump's tweet was not an isolated event, and it was lent authenticity by Trump having been baiting Kim for months. It was also posted without deliberation or advice, and in ignorance of the actual state of affairs. This might have been a feature of Trump's tweeting in reality, but it is a practice that others are unlikely to follow. The issue in this fictional account was not so much the use of Twitter but the ability of a leader to make an inflammatory statement without heeding advice or having their bureaucracy prepare for the consequences.

In an example of an actual tweet with an unintentionally escalatory effect, in August 2018 Canadian foreign minister Chrystia Freeland responded to the arrest of Saudi human-rights activist Samar Badawi:

> Very alarmed to learn that Samar Badawi, Raif Badawi's sister, has been imprisoned in Saudi Arabia. Canada stands together with the Badawi family in this difficult time, and we continue to strongly call for the release of both Raif and Samar Badawi.[16]

The tweet, aimed at a Canadian domestic audience, had international repercussions because Riyadh considered it insulting and provocative. It provoked a furious Saudi response that included expelling the Canadian ambassador, threatening to freeze all new trade and investment, halting flights between the countries, and recalling Saudi students studying in Canada. Iyad Madani, a former Saudi information minister, wrote that Canada was interfering in his country's domestic affairs: 'Canada blundered because it seems to have ignored and forgotten that civil society and political social development are best left to the dynamics of each society.'[17] Ultimately, Canada did not back down and not all the Saudi threats were implemented.

Twitter in context

While Twitter remains the social-media platform most used for political statements and for individuals to access news, it is not necessarily more significant than print and broadcast media in the formation of national narratives.[18] Public attitudes at times of crisis are also shaped by older mediums, including television news networks, radio shows and even old-fashioned newspapers. Trump's political rise, for example, owed as much to Fox News as to Twitter. But Twitter, and social media more generally, does have advantages over other forms of political communication in that an individual's messages can reach a wide audience directly and at great speed. It is easy to access, and accounts are free to create. It makes available multiple and diverse sources of news and analysis to wide audiences and across national boundaries.

Twitter opened for business in 2006, two years after Facebook and a year before Apple launched the iPhone. Its use expanded as smartphones became more common – in 2022 there were some 6.6 billion smartphones in use worldwide, accounting for 80% of all social-media traffic – and according to most estimates there are now more than 370 million Twitter users worldwide.[19] The greatest number of them are in the US (about 65m), followed by Japan (52m), Brazil (17m), the United Kingdom (16m) and India (15m).[20] The platform is currently blocked in China, Iran and North Korea.

The world's third-most visited website, after Google and YouTube, Facebook is even broader in its reach than Twitter, with almost 3bn monthly users in the first quarter of 2023.[21] In the US it is the most popular social-media platform and a regular source of news for more than 30% of adults.[22] Whereas open social-media platforms such as Twitter provide users with the opportunity to interact with strangers, closed platforms such as Facebook, VKontakte and WhatsApp allow users to communicate with people they already know and trust.[23]

After initially presenting their platforms as facilitating almost any content that users wished to post, social-media companies and administrators later sought to respond to concerns that this equated to encouraging dangerous and often fake information. Facebook introduced fact-checking policies with the goal of ensuring that shared material was correct and accurate and did not mislead other users.[24] Twitter moved in 2020 to remove fake accounts and bots and to prevent inflammatory tweets, especially those that might damage public health by spreading false information about the COVID-19 pandemic. Following Musk's purchase of Twitter in October 2022, some of these safeguards were removed, and Trump's account was reinstated. Musk's arrival as CEO underscored existing questions about the role of private individuals with the ability to manipulate and control the digital information space, working for profit or personal gain.

A similar issue was raised in October 2021 when the 'Facebook Papers' were released, including revelations by whistle-blower Frances Haugen. A particularly striking revelation was that although Facebook CEO Mark Zuckerberg had told the US Congress in 2020 that Facebook was managing to remove 94% of hate speech on the platform, internal documents showed the true figure was less than 5%.[25] Hate speech noticeably proliferated in the lead-up to elections and during crises, such as the 2019 India–Pakistan crisis. The papers revealed that one of Facebook's troubling features is the 'filter bubble', whereby algorithms consistently feed users more of the same information, creating potentially dangerous echo chambers of misinformation and disinformation.[26] The company also prioritised 'clicks' over content and would either fail to censor popular individuals and messages or would censor content at the request of a popular individual. As a result, the company and its standards mechanism, XCheck, shielded high-profile individuals, many of whom then used Facebook to spread disinformation or to harass others.[27] Despite numerous internal efforts to suppress incendiary posts, the company baulked at content management because of its commitment to neutrality and because it might impede growth.[28]

In 2021, members of Myanmar's Rohingya Muslim minority sued Facebook for US$150bn over its alleged role in facilitating genocide, which supposedly included its algorithms amplifying hate speech. Facebook acknowledged in 2018 that it had been negligent in preventing incitement against the Rohingya, noting that 'Facebook has become a means for those seeking to spread hate and cause harm, and posts have been linked to offline violence'.[29] However, genocide has never been dependent on innovative means of communication. The Rwanda genocide of 1994, for example, which was exacerbated by eliminationist rhetoric broadcast by radio, suggests caution should be applied to any judgement that social media plays a unique role in inciting murderous behaviour.

Crisis management in the digital environment

These developments in communications and technology coincided with geopolitical shifts in which China and Russia emerged as strategic adversaries of the Western powers. Strategic reviews by the UK and the US pointed to the need to manage complex multi-domain crises, in which information operations were expected to be an important component. The UK's 2021 Integrated Review, for example, stated that

> technology will create new vulnerabilities to hostile activity and attack in domains such as cyberspace and space, notably including the spread of disinformation online. It will undermine social cohesion, community and national identity as individuals spend more time in a virtual world and as automation reshapes the labour market.[30]

In the same year, the analyst Margaret Marangione warned of Russia's and China's ability to use information operations to exploit groups and individuals, and called for a strengthening of 'cognitive security'.[31] The effect of information campaigns may be more acute during international crises, when tensions are high, information might be scarce and time is short. A 2021 report by the Center for Strategic and International Studies, for example, described 'tactics such as hack and leak operations, forgeries, elite or media co-optation, including flash mobs, bribery, coercion and intimidation, flooding the information zone, false flag operations, causing chaos to provide cover for riskier influence operations, and microtargeting', and argued that 'in periods of crisis or conflict, the escalatory potential of such activities may be higher while patterns and pathways of escalation involving influence operations may evade the step-based and comparatively linear expectations for escalation and crisis management so prevalent among national security deci-sionmakers'.[32] The 2023 'refresh' of the UK's Integrated Review reported that the Department for Science, Innovation and Technology's Counter Disinformation Unit 'will continue to work with both social media platforms and our allies to improve our understanding of the different techniques used in malicious information operations and our ability to counter them, including through the use of intelligence declassification'.[33]

To examine the potential escalatory (or de-escalatory) effect of digital information campaigns on international crises, we first develop a framework for thinking about their interaction. This considers the various types of narrative deployed online during crises and how they might affect crisis-management options. We then examine the role of information campaigns in four recent crises: India–Pakistan, 2019; US–Iran, 2020; China's use of social media during the COVID-19 pandemic, 2020–22; and the conflict in Ukraine from 2013 until the full-blown war following Russia's invasion in 2022. We intentionally selected cases involving at least one nuclear actor, and crises that had potential to escalate or significantly shift the geopolitical landscape (although obviously the COVID-19 case lacked a military dimension and the death toll was not due to deliberate violence). We conclude by examining trends across the case studies and look ahead to how these might affect future crises. In so doing, we raise concerns about certain trends, including authoritarian actors that rely on social media to spread anti-democratic narratives, using increasingly sophisticated mechanisms; the potential for domestic audiences to become radicalised; and the possibility of information designed for one audience being misinterpreted by another.

Five findings emerge from our analysis of the case studies:

1. Information campaigns, including those on social media, are only one part of wider political struggles shaped by various influential instruments of power. A tweet alone cannot escalate a crisis. Rather, at times of crisis, information campaigns interact with other, more traditional forms of military and economic power.

2. The ease with which public perceptions can be shifted by information campaigns should not be exaggerated, especially when they come from foreign or anonymous sources and challenge established narratives. Crisis messages are likely to be most effective with domestic audiences, where they are likely to reinforce existing views.

3. States cannot therefore be confident that information campaigns will have the desired effects. While conventional wisdom suggests that states such as Russia and China have taken full advantage of the digital environment to advance their information campaigns – and we do not doubt the extent of this effort – there is little hard evidence that they have made much material difference. To the extent that they have done so, it was because they aggravated existing problems in the target society (as with the interference in the 2016 US presidential election – the most commonly cited example of success).

4. Information campaigns are limited as strategic instruments because of the difficulty of anticipating the effects that messages will have, even when sent by a political leader. Messages can be interpreted in different ways, and audiences also vary.

5. Social-media campaigns are also hard to control. This is the case even with domestic audiences. They can, for example, create a 'rally round the flag' effect that could have unintended international consequences by increasing domestic pressure on an authoritarian leader to escalate.

Two of our findings require additional emphasis. Firstly, many state-led digital information campaigns, such as those of China and Russia, are largely focused on reinforcing narratives among their domestic audiences and have little impact abroad – with important exceptions such as Russia's interference in the 2016 US election, which successfully rein-forced existing tensions in the target country. Secondly, the use of digital information campaigns in the cases we examined were not 'like war', as some analysts have characterised the phenomenon, but rather were part of the broader geopolitical picture involving economic and political factors that ultimately determined campaign success or failure.[34] The novel technol-ogy of social-media platforms might change the way that leaders communicate during a crisis, but the impact of digital information campaigns needs to be considered in context. It remains the case, even in the digital age, that the most impor-tant elements determining how crises are managed are the political stakes, along with material factors including military options and economic risks. We do not argue that information campaigns, including the introduction of fake news and mali-cious rumours, are irrelevant and can have no harmful effects. There is always a possibility that a particular message might have a disproportionate impact, which is why this is an area that needs watching with care. But these effects may be less severe than often feared because, in recent years, there has been an increasing awareness of the pernicious form these campaigns can take and the importance of counteracting them.

CHAPTER ONE

Understanding narratives and information campaigns

This chapter considers the relationship between digital information campaigns and strategic narratives. Our framework is based on distinctions between 'formal', 'issue' and 'legitimacy' narratives, as well as those between 'offensive' and 'defensive' information campaigns.

We should first distinguish information campaigns or information operations in the digital age from 'cyber operations', 'cyber attacks' or 'offensive cyber'. The latter involve the use of digital networks either to obtain intelligence or to mount direct attacks on the adversary's infrastructure and its general ability to function. In more old-fashioned parlance, these activities would be described as 'espionage' or 'sabotage'. Their targets are likely to be found in government or corporate networks, or in elements of critical infrastructure such as energy supplies, transport and financial services. With information operations, we are more concerned with 'propaganda' and possibly 'subversion': the use of information to advance a political message. The goal of such activities is to bolster narratives already supporting state policies or to target those of critics or adversary governments, aiming to deprive them of credibility. In *Like War: The Weaponization of Social*

Media, Peter Singer and Emerson Brooking distinguish cyber operations from information operations by describing the former as being about hacking *networks* and the latter being about hacking the *people* on those networks.[1] There is also an obvious difference between activities that can cause immediate material harm and those that are about changing social and political attitudes.

In practice, of course, cyber and information operations can intertwine. For example, Russia's 'hack and leak' operation against the US Democratic Party in 2016 began with a cyber intrusion into the Democratic National Committee's network and Democratic operatives' email accounts. This was followed by the dissemination of the stolen information via WikiLeaks in order to influence the outcome of the 2016 US presidential election. Some might label this an 'offensive cyber operation'.[2] Our analysis focuses not on how information is itself obtained in the digital environment, but on how states use it to advance narratives, and the strategic significance of that use.

It is now widely assumed that information campaigns run through social media are having a transformational effect on how international conflicts are managed. Singer and Brooking argue that information operations in the digital age can change the course of elections and even military battles:

> Social networks also create new ways to reach out and attack, even from thousands of miles away. Propagandists can identify a few dozen sympathizers out of a faraway population of millions and then groom them to attack their fellow citizens. Voices from around the globe can stir the pot of hatred and resentment between rival peoples, sparking a war or genocide. They can even divide and conquer a country's politics from afar, realizing the political objective of a war without firing a shot.[3]

Like others, they identified Russia as the master of this form of warfare – 'reaping the rewards of being ahead of the game … using its online strength to substitute for declining military power'.[4] The American analyst Seth Jones, for example, has shown the evolving role of 'information warfare' in Russian, Iranian and Chinese strategic thinking and how it was embraced as a means of disrupting and disorienting their opponents.[5]

The increased use of information campaigns is a consequence not only of the supposed ease with which these can now be mounted but also of increased awareness of the risks attached to open conflict. Much of the interest in both cyber and information campaigns stemmed from the assumption that states would prefer to pursue their objectives by means short of all-out war. These could include a range of non-violent forms of coercion, such as hostile resolutions at the UN Security Council, travel restrictions on individuals, sports boycotts, economic sanctions, energy cut-offs and withdrawal of foreign aid. China, for example, has increasingly been flexing its muscles by using threats to withdraw access to its markets in an attempt to discourage criticism of its practices in foreign media and academia. Recent examples include its ban on imports of Canadian canola oil after the arrest of Meng Wanzhou, threats to boycott H&M when it refused to buy cotton from Xinjiang, and attempts at various forms of economic coercion reflecting its displeasure at Australia.[6] Information campaigns are thus only one example of a range of measures used to operate in what has been described as a 'grey zone' between peace and war. It may be that the current Russia–Ukraine war will confirm the advantages of staying in the grey zone; it already demonstrates that one context for information campaigns can be open warfare, when the stakes are much higher.

Social media and strategic narratives

If these campaigns are influential, it will be because of their impact on 'strategic narratives', an area that has gained increasing attention in recent years.[7] Most policy discourse takes a narrative form, as stories provide a means by which we make sense of the world and our place in it. Strategic narratives enable parties in a conflict to explain the interests at stake and why their pursuit has taken a particular form. Coercive strategies require explanations about why certain measures are being applied and what the target must do to get them removed. Resorting to armed force requires demonstrating to those making the sacrifices how a more terrible fate is being averted or how a better peace should result. Support for another state or those rebelling against that state requires explaining why this is deserved and the difference it might make. Vast expenditures on military preparedness, threats of war designed to deter, and the choice of allies and enemies: all must be justified. This is why 'narratives' have come to be stressed in discussions about contemporary strategy, and in considerations of the role of social media.[8] Narratives provide the storylines of conflict and in doing so become an arena of conflict themselves. When states mount information campaigns against other countries, they are trying to change the narrative.

Our categorisation of narratives depends on their intent. *Formal* narratives are authoritative official statements and as such can be tools of open diplomacy. *Issue* narratives develop around specific policies or crises, while *legitimacy* narratives are about the sources of an actor's authority, and so may be required to shore up political leadership.

Formal narratives, and the messages intended to reinforce them, convey the agreed views of organisations, including governments. They can be assessed as authoritative statements. What matters here is not whether these storylines are well developed or convincing but whether they can be attributed directly to the leadership of an organisation or government. Formal narratives are set out in official communications. They might include explanations of why a situation is of concern, what remedies are expected, and conditional threats indicating what might happen if appropriate steps are not taken. This is the business of diplomacy and considerable effort goes into crafting formal narratives. Multiple audiences must be addressed, all of whom must be expected to read and interpret words carefully. For this reason, official pronouncements may be ambiguous and convoluted. Formal narratives are especially important when it comes to crisis management. They must always be taken seriously, and will be studied carefully for the most subtle changes of position during times of crisis.

Issue narratives cover a contentious area of policy that may not be directly relevant to the way a country is governed. Issue narratives can be employed to justify entering or staying out of a war. Examples are the role of the 'yellow press' leading up to the Spanish–American War; the massive effort the British put into getting Americans 'on side' in 1940–41; the demands of leftist movements in arguing for a 'second front' to ease the Soviet Union's position in 1942; and the arguments over why the US was fighting in Vietnam, or later in Iraq and Afghanistan. Issues that have been poorly handled can escalate, turning into legitimacy narratives that challenge the government responsible. This is likely to be truer for issues of war and peace than for domestic questions.

Legitimacy narratives are not new. Getting large numbers of people to think in particular ways has long been identified as a vital source of power – from well before the digital age – and are a means of preserving the position of an elite, making it appear that its position is part of the natural order of things. Radical theorists have looked for ways to undermine this 'false consciousness' by drawing attention to inequalities and injustice, and then trying to persuade the masses to imagine a better and more just society.[9]

All three types of narrative can be categorised as either offensive or defensive. *Offensive* information campaigns are more ambitious in their aims of changing how people think and injecting a new narrative that challenges pre-existing views. They are typically revisionist in nature and focused on changing minds and shifting current thinking. *Defensive* information campaigns, conversely, are focused on reinforcing pre-existing views. Defensive campaigns are often, but not always, targeted at domestic audiences to maintain the status quo.

There are important differences between authoritarian and liberal states when it comes to their own narratives and those of others. When it comes to formal narratives, liberal states accept that the information environment cannot be wholly controlled and that therefore they must largely rely on the quality of their own narratives and their ability to counter those they deem harmful on their own terms. Because liberal systems facilitate peaceful transfers of power, they do not generally consider the legitimacy of their form of government to be at stake. Their focus will be much more on specific issues.

Authoritarian regimes wish to control their information environment and have a low tolerance of dissident opinions, relying on censorship and repression. Because direct challenges are often considered threatening, authoritarian states will see a greater risk of an issue narrative – in which they are challenged about the handling of a specific matter – turning into a legitimacy narrative, whereby the whole power structure is challenged. They are apt to see any sort of challenge as potentially subversive.

Each new form of communication has had an impact on political conduct and the dominant narratives. Subversive groups since the fifteenth century have relied on secret printing presses and pamphlets. At first, radio benefitted authoritarian governments because they could shut down competitors, reach into rural areas and be heard by the illiterate. Later they would put great effort into jamming the BBC World Service, which was able to challenge official narratives simply by providing trusted news and commentary. Ayatollah Ruhollah Khomeini challenged Shah Reza Pahlavi in 1978 with cassette tapes distributed through Iranian mosques. Tuning in to West German TV made East Germans aware of a more attractive way of life during the Cold War.

What has been the effect of the most recent information revolution – the spread of social media – over the past two decades? Much of the early discussion of the political impact of social media focused less on the ability of states to influence public opinion elsewhere than on the degree to which individuals and non-governmental groups could be empowered. According to the journalist David Patrikarakos, 'this empowerment of the individual – the creation of *Homo digitalis* – is at the heart of twenty-first-century conflict'.[10] Protesters during the Arab Spring, for example, took advantage of social-media platforms to challenge autocratic regimes and increase international awareness of their cause.[11] Similarly, although they were ultimately unsuccessful, social media catalysed anti-regime protests in Iran in 2009 and in Russia in 2011–13. This development was not, of course, confined to liberal movements. Insurgent groups such as the Islamic State (ISIS) also used social media for recruiting and directing propaganda blasts at their opponents to unnerve them and weaken their resolve. While rebel movements challenged the legitimacy of states, other non-governmental organisations concentrated on specific issues.[12] For example, Bellingcat, an open-source investigation team founded by Eliot Higgins, drew on social-media evidence when investigating how a Russian *Buk* anti-aircraft missile shot down Malaysia Airlines flight MH17 over Ukraine on 17 July 2014. The Bellingcat team relied on various social-media platforms and other open-source tools to track the missile from Russia to Ukraine. The digitisation of information makes it more widely available to the public, and those willing to put in the time can uncover government secrets.

Yet while there was an early expectation that ubiquitous access to the internet would subvert authoritarian regimes, and some early indications that this might be the case, those regimes have fought back. The Chinese government has made strenuous efforts to regulate the internet for purposes of social control. It denies its citizens access to Western-controlled media and insists that they use only its own approved platforms, behind what has become known as the 'Great Firewall'. This is all essentially defensive, relying on censorship, concealment and deception. While authoritarian regimes may be more vulnerable to a demonstrable failure in a political crisis or a military operation, they may also be better placed to prevent awkward facts or adverse commentaries becoming part of the national discourse. In this respect authoritarian regimes are at an advantage because liberal regimes are more restrained in their efforts to censor, control or cut off social media.[13] As we show in Chapter Four on Beijing's handling of the coronavirus pandemic, though, such methods have their limits.

At the same time, Western platforms are easy to access and so provide a relatively inexpensive and straightforward way to mount assaults on the narratives of liberal states and to push alternative views of reality. There is thus an asymmetry of opportunity in the current situation. That is one reason why Western commentators tend to see information campaigns mounted through social media as a threat. Yet many of the information campaigns that authoritarian regimes have used against liberal democracies appear defensive, designed to bolster the position of authoritarian national elites. This may involve making claims that appear as palpable nonsense outside the home country but work well enough inside.

Singer and Brooking suggest that information campaigns can be carried out using special tactics to achieve 'clicks, interactions, engagement, and immersion time' from the target audience. The trick is to make messages 'go viral'. The most successful information warriors are those who understand how to do this by using 'narrative, emotion, authenticity, community, inundation, and experimentation'. They argue that

> these wars are won by those able to shape the story lines that frame public understanding, to provoke the responses that impel people to action, to connect with a plurality of followers at the most personal level, to build a sense of fellowship, and to do it all on a global scale, again and again, but using individual reaction to each attack as a moment for mass refinement.[14]

But this is a demanding challenge, especially when the objective is offensive – that is, to change the way people already think – rather than defensive, when the aim is to reinforce existing views.

The mixed results of digital information campaigns

Social-media platforms lend themselves to information campaigns. Digital information campaigns have become a routine feature of political affairs, including international conflicts. Yet despite the relative ease and modest cost of mounting them, their effectiveness remains uncertain. It depends on a multitude of factors – for example economic and cultural ones, along with the vagaries of individual perception – which make their success unpredictable. There are many complexities relating to how opinions are formed; to the divergence between what the senders believe their messages to mean and what is actually received and interpreted; and to whether narratives 'stick' or are ephemeral.

In Western countries, governments are open to regular challenge and at any time there may be a range of often intense debates and controversies. That is before any interference from foreigners. In such a cacophonous environment it is not easy for a new narrative to become established to the point where it has a measurable effect. When narratives do make a difference, this is likely to be in connection with a particular event, such as an election or a major policy announcement, or possibly in relation to an ongoing international crisis.

There is a substantial literature on the construction of credible narratives, much of it from before the digital age.[15] From this we learn that the most effective narratives derive organically from national cultures and tradition and have a sufficient connection to credible evidence or lived experience to be plausible. Some might appeal only to narrow sections of a society because they require a leap of faith or a conspiratorial approach to evidence. Others might be constructed with such ingenuity that they can cope with unwelcome new information, apparent inconsistencies or loose ends.

The literature on cognition warns that challenging established narratives is not easy. Human minds can deploy a variety of heuristics to help them cope with or deflect uncomfortable information. They can be resistant to clever storytelling, especially if the story is told by a potential enemy, a member of a rival political camp, or just someone there is no reason to trust. It is simpler to reinforce existing narratives or adapt them to new circumstances than to replace them with something entirely new. Our case-study evidence suggests that defensive information campaigns, designed to reinforce established narratives, are more likely to succeed than offensive campaigns, which are designed to disrupt an established position. Moreover, research suggests that social media tends to reinforce pre-existing views in its users, who often fall into echo chambers. Individuals predisposed to a particular view of the world are likely to stick with their initial stances even when exposed to alternative perspectives.[16] In general, the safest assumption is that social-media messages are as likely to reinforce as to challenge existing power structures and beliefs. Digital information campaigns can influence political relationships, but the main drivers of change will still be events that disrupt everyday lives, whether financial crises, pandemics or wars.

An analogy with cyber operations can be helpful in understanding the limitations of information operations. In an examination of the effectiveness of cyber attacks, Lennart Maschmeyer notes that they often fall short of expectations because of what he calls the 'subversive trilemma'. Subversion relies on 'the secret exploitation of vulnerabilities in a system of rules'. It works by using an adversary's own capabilities against its own systems in order to, for example, turn public opinion, degrade material capabilities or undermine institutional efficiency. The advantage of subversion is that it makes possible an intervention in an adversary's affairs that is less costly and risky than physical warfare. Yet it is less effective than often supposed because of the same factors that make it a tempting instrument of influence. It must be secret and indirect, so it requires a significant effort to be established and maintained. This limits the speed with which cyber operations can be implemented, their intensity and the ability to control effects. Maschmeyer describes this as a trilemma because a gain in one of these three aspects (speed, say) tends to come at the expense of the other two (in this case intensity and control).[17]

Information campaigns, which seek to change perceptions and opinions that are already subject to many influences, are also vulnerable to the subversive trilemma. If the campaign originates from another country, it may be less credible and effective than one that appears to be homegrown, so there is the same advantage in avoiding attribution as with cyber operations; but, similarly, efforts to conceal and deceive may also limit the intensity of the campaign and make it harder to control its consequences.

Maschmeyer's subversive trilemma helps us consider the inherent tensions between the assumption that offensive information campaigns will be more effective if their origins are hidden, the need to develop the narrative quickly in response to events, and the challenge of keeping the narrative under control once it has been launched and might be picked up and developed, as well as refuted, by other actors. When outside interventions are unable to draw upon strong local themes, they are often relatively easy to spot, poorly executed and have little effect. Russia seemed to realise this was an issue with its information campaigns around the 2014 invasion of Ukraine, and hired locals to check disinformation for contextual accuracy.[18] Moreover, because of what happened in the 2016 US presidential election, sensitivity to potential interference is greater – indeed, before the 2020 election, much of the US media was so aware of the possibility that it might be the victim of another Russian disinformation campaign that it largely ignored or discredited reports relating to President Joe Biden's son, even though later investigations suggested that at least some of the embarrassing materials in question were in fact genuine.[19] The 2020 presidential and 2022 midterm elections were watched carefully, with little foreign interference reported.

Though the impact of foreign information campaigns is hard to identify, this does not mean it is negligible. It has been reported that some companies discreetly advertise their ability to mount digital disinformation campaigns in elections world-wide.[20] After all, in elections that are being decided by fine margins it might not take much for a campaign to have a dispro-portionate effect. But even in cases where there is an impact, it might be relatively small or even counterproductive from the perspective of the perpetrators. To the extent that Trump's presidency caused wider divisions within the Western alliance, his election might have been of some benefit to Moscow, but the suspicion that it had interfered on his behalf inhibited his ability to adopt a pro-Moscow policy and led to his opponents distrusting Russia even more than before.

It is therefore difficult to isolate the specific impact of digital information campaigns, just as it was with those conducted through the print and broadcast media, because their effects will depend on their interaction with a range of other factors. This is particularly true at the 'high end' of international affairs, where decisions on war and peace are made and crises might escalate or de-escalate. These matters have already been studied in depth elsewhere. Our starting point therefore should be our established understanding of contemporary international affairs and strategic practice. With any given crisis this might lead to certain expectations about its likely outcome, which provides one yardstick against which to measure the impact of an information campaign.

Digital narratives and crisis management

Our position on 'narrative warfare' is similar to that adopted by Thomas Rid concerning 'cyber war', which he argued would not take place because the effects of these capabilities depended on their interaction with the harder forms of power. In this respect we could say that 'Twitter war' will not take place either.[21] Although social media is the tool for contemporary digital information campaigns that people are most aware of and interact with most regularly, it does not play a vital or original role in inter-state communications during crises. It has not replaced more traditional means of diplomatic or crisis communication, whether through back channels or dialogues. Where it is used for crisis communication it is not notably more effective than more traditional means. Crises continue to be influenced by a confluence of factors, including traditional military issues such as symmetry or asymmetry of forces, and political ones including the stakes at risk. A tweet alone cannot start a nuclear war and the wider context is what ultimately shapes crisis dynamics and whether or not they escalate or de-escalate.

The most substantial impact of digital information campaigns during crises will almost always be on support at home. In this respect information operations are typically defensive, focused on reinforcing pre-existing views about leadership and national interests with domestic audiences, who will appreciate and be more receptive to the messages. In general, information operations are more effective in appealing to and amplifying pre-existing narratives than in creating new ones. Shifting opinion in a target country is difficult unless it is already shifting. It is the divisions that are causing these shifts that might then be amplified by shrewd messaging. In states where the media is heavily censored, campaigns will face little competition. In regions where there is competition for influence – Africa, for example – success in promoting the benefits of staying friendly with Russia or China will depend on evidence of tangible assistance, for example through economic aid or COVID-19 vaccines. Information campaigns do not work in isolation.

Moments of crisis, when states may be acting in ways that challenge international norms or create unexpected dangers, are when settled narratives might be challenged. At these times there will be intense public and governmental interest in the latest news, and urgent debates about the meaning of particular events and appropriate responses. In what may appear to be a unique and dynamic set of circumstances, in a highly competitive information environment, key actors will be anxious to impose their narratives but might struggle to do so. They may be more vulnerable to rumours that by their nature will be difficult to substantiate, and to the sudden emergence of new and desperate narratives fed from numerous sources in an environment where it is hard to work out exactly what is going on – for example following a terrorist attack, act of sabotage, attempted assassination or reports of troop movements. Officials may be checking their smartphones instead of waiting for confirmation of events through official channels.

If military action is in the offing, there may be a 'rally round the flag' effect that will boost the attention given to formal narratives and the public's readiness to believe them. At such times the government will wish to maximise influence over all narratives, especially those that relate to operational secrecy. Yet this will be difficult because of the ease with which images and messages can be shared with wider audiences. There will also be concern about Photoshopped or falsified images, relying on 'deep fake' technology. As has been seen in the Russia–Ukraine war, even governments that wish to impose strict censorship find it difficult to control reports from the front lines enabled by new technologies, meaning that military operations are much more transparent than they were in the past. The internet is now used to identify targets by terrorists, insurgents and invading armies, as well as those countering them.

One consequence of situations in which there may be more propaganda, rumour and fakery than usual is that formal narratives become even more important. Pronouncements by leading political figures will achieve rapid and widespread transmission, and will soon be noticed in foreign capitals. They will be interrogated for nuances and hidden meanings. They will be assumed to be the most authoritative evidence of a government's approach to crisis management. If they are threatening in detail and tone, they can be a potential source of escalation; if calming and conciliatory, or even hinting at areas of compromise, they can be de-escalatory. An obvious difficulty with official communications is that of multiple audiences: messages largely intended for internal consumption are hard to distinguish from those intended for an international audience. The former might be designed to boost morale and maintain national unity while the latter will be attempting to control the processes of escalation, which might involve threats capable of alarming their domestic audience or conciliatory messages that might irritate hardliners. This problem, which is again not novel in international crises, is likely to be aggravated in situations in which statements reach domestic and international audiences at the same time. It becomes much harder to tailor messages for a specific audience when they can be immediately read by anyone.

The fact that messages designed for one audience will be picked up by others is why information campaigns, particularly in the digital age, can be hard to control. It is difficult to confine their reception to one section of local opinion, or just domestic audiences, or just one set of external actors. Even when a foreign audience is the target of a campaign, the message received may not be the one intended. A public threat by a foreign government to take firm action, for example, might be intended to influence the target government by causing alarm and even panic among sections of its population, but such threats might also instil a popular mood of defiance and resistance. It is a familiar problem with all communications, especially across cultures and political systems, that the meaning attached to messages by those sending them is not how they are received, and that even if they are understood as intended, they still do not necessarily change behaviour as anticipated.

We can also envision circumstances in which a nationalistic government finds itself in a geopolitical crisis and adopts inflammatory rhetoric that leads to a strong domestic reaction, with calls for violence and escalation.[22] If at some point the government then wishes to de-escalate the crisis, its options may be seriously limited by nationalist pressure and it might even be forced into tougher action to appease domestic audiences. In such a scenario, narratives advanced on social media could have a self-reinforcing and ultimately hand-tying effect. Again, however, this is not a new dynamic. It could be seen, for example, after Argentina's occupation of the Falkland Islands in 1982, when the popularity of the move made it difficult for the ruling military junta to offer concessions during negotiations intended to find a peaceful solution to the crisis. Another, and possibly more germane, example would be the anti-Japanese riots that broke out in some 30 Chinese cities in April 2005, which involved violence against Japanese-brand cars and stores, following the Japanese prime minister's public refusal to stop visiting the controversial Yasukuni shrine. Eventually the Chinese government had to step in to restore order.[23] This is another example of the core problem with information campaigns, whether digital or analogue: once started they are difficult to control.

The case studies in the next four chapters show, in different ways, the importance states attach to shaping narratives at times of crisis, and how the importance of those narratives in sustaining domestic support is rarely matched by the states' ability to influence the attitudes of their rivals and adversaries.

CHAPTER TWO

India–Pakistan, 2019

On 27 February 2019, the most popular tweet in the world was a call for peace using the hashtag '#Saynotowar'. The hashtag was prompted by an escalating crisis between India and Pakistan over the long-contested region of Kashmir. The crisis began with a terrorist attack on Indian paramilitary forces in Kashmir on 14 February, and concluded after two weeks of conflict including airstrikes and troop deployments. Crisis management, especially on the Indian side, was influenced by the imminence of the general elections that would take place in India in April and May. Throughout the crisis India claimed Pakistan was behind the initial terrorist attack. It retaliated on 26 February with an airstrike on an alleged terrorist camp in Pakistan. The crisis eventually eased following the return of a captured Indian pilot on 1 March, though thereafter the Indian government tightened its control over Kashmir.

During the crisis and in its aftermath, most of the social-media activity came from domestic actors in India, particularly in the lead-up to the elections in April and May. The ruling Bharatiya Janata Party (BJP) and its supporters used the crisis to reinforce a domestic narrative that it was more effective at countering terrorism than the rival Congress Party, along with an international narrative that India remained a victim of Pakistani-supported terrorism. These narratives were constructed and delivered through a variety of social-media platforms, spread by hundreds of thousands of BJP-affiliated volunteers, and took on a particularly nationalist and occasionally violent tone in many closed platforms, such as WhatsApp,[1] along with calls on Twitter to attack Kashmiris and 'shoot the traitors'.[2] Indeed, subsequent revelations about Facebook's inner workings showed that it failed to shut down hate speech and calls for violence during the crisis and in the lead-up to the elections.[3] Perhaps more so than any other case study, this one raises questions about the quality of the administration of social media.

The BJP's use of social media during and after the crisis was aimed at advancing self-serving narratives through seemingly independent actors. To a large extent this was motivated by domestic electoral concerns rather than a desire to influence Pakistani calculations. While this domestic information campaign amplified nationalist and violent messages within India, there is little evidence that it had a major effect on raising or lowering the level of tension between India and Pakistan. Indeed, a paradox of this case is that the bellicose domestic messaging and inflated claims of military success gave Prime Minister Modi sufficient political space to de-escalate the crisis. This demonstrates that there is not necessarily a simple crossover from domestic messaging to international effects. Nonetheless, while it may not always be the case, the more virulent domestic campaigns can contribute to a more volatile nationalist political environment that makes future crises harder to resolve.

The lead-up to the crisis: tensions in Kashmir and the stability–instability paradox

Kashmir has been a flashpoint in India–Pakistan relations since partition in 1947. After the religiously diverse region was given the option of joining either India or Pakistan, regional leader Hari Singh agreed to join India in 1947 in the wake of an invasion by Pakistani forces.[4] In 1948 the two sides agreed to a ceasefire line separating their territories. Later, under the Simla Agreement that followed the 1971 war, this became the Line of Control (LoC), which has served as a de facto border ever since. Although there has not been another full-scale war since 1971, the Simla Agreement did not end the tension between the two countries.

In 1998 the stakes became much higher when both countries tested nuclear weapons. The danger became apparent the next year with a conflict, commonly known as the Kargil War, when Pakistani troops infiltrated across the LoC and occupied territory. At the time, Kargil was part of the division of Ladakh, which was itself part of the province of Jammu and Kashmir, and had been under Indian control since partition. In 1999, following this Pakistani incursion, India responded by launching a military offensive. This prompted active international engagement led by US president Bill Clinton. The conflict ended with an effective defeat for the Pakistani forces, which were withdrawn. During the conflict, when Indian forces had attacked Pakistani positions on the Indian side of the LoC, Pakistan responded by moving its nuclear weapons from storage and threatening to use 'any weapon in its arsenal to protect its territorial integrity'.[5]

A variety of factors contributed to the de-escalation of the Kargil crisis. American intervention to negotiate a ceasefire was certainly important. In addition, Pakistan failed to anticipate the international opprobrium and response to its actions.[6]

A military explanation is that India was conventionally superior and used airpower to effectively deliver firepower and force Pakistan's withdrawal.[7] In a comprehensive study on types of crises, Mark Bell and Julia Macdonald argue that Kargil was a 'staircase crisis', which 'exhibited incentives for first nuclear use' but where 'the level of escalation was relatively controllable by the leaders involved'. Further escalation was avoided through a combination of Indian command and control, Pakistani red lines, and communication channels that proved effective during the crisis.[8] Deterrence was a factor, as both states were wary of their adversary's nuclear capability.

This reflects what has been described as the 'stability–instability paradox', whereby the presence of nuclear weapons deters escalation and creates stability at the strategic level but creates greater instability at lower levels of conflict. Michael Krepon described the stability–instability paradox in the context of South Asia:

> One central tenet of the stability–instability paradox – that offsetting nuclear capabilities will increase tensions between adversaries – has already been amply demonstrated in South Asia. While India's difficulties in Kashmir are rooted in poor governance and domestic grievances, Pakistan's active support for separatism and militancy in Kashmir has notably coincided with its acquisition of covert nuclear capabilities. Tensions between India and Pakistan have intensified further since both nations tested nuclear weapons in 1998. A nuclearized subcontinent has already produced a succession of nuclear-tinged crises and one conflict that was limited in time, space, as well as in the choice of weapons used.[9]

The incentives to avoid nuclear exchange also encourage efforts to operate in the grey zone using methods short of war, including information campaigns, to seek strategic advantage while managing risks.

New Delhi and Islamabad again came close to war in the crisis following a terrorist attack on the Indian parliament in December 2001, which Indian officials said was supported by Pakistan. There were various phases of escalation and de-escalation during the following year, including the mobilisation of both countries' armed forces. In 2008, terrorist attacks in Mumbai revived concerns over the danger of uncontrolled escalation. And again in 2016, both sides' armed forces went on high alert following a series of anti-Indian protests in Kashmir after a militia leader was killed. On 18 September 2016, a group of Jaish-e-Mohammed (JeM) terrorists attacked an Indian military base and killed 17 soldiers. In response, Modi initially threatened to cut off the water supply to Pakistan, but then launched a series of strikes into Pakistani territory instead. Pakistan denied the strikes ever occurred. This crisis, like the Kargil conflict in 1999, abated. However, since Modi's election as prime minister in 2014, a pattern had been established in India–Pakistan tensions over Kashmir: militants or terrorists would attack Indian targets in the region; India would accuse Pakistan of supporting the attacks, and retaliate militarily. It was a pattern the 2019 crisis would follow.

In the run-up to the crisis there was a significant gap between Indians and Pakistanis in their use of social media, and that has remained the case. According to a February 2021 report, 624m Indians were using social media, or nearly half the population, with Facebook, YouTube and WhatsApp the most popular platforms.[10] Between 2018 and 2021 the number of Facebook users in India more than doubled, from 190m to 402m.[11] Modi is one of the most popular politicians on social media, including Twitter and YouTube, in terms of both followers and engagement by users. Conversely, in January 2021 there were only 46m social-media users in Pakistan, just 20% of the population.[12] But Pakistani political leaders, such as former prime minister Imran Khan, are active on social media and have used it to advance their messages and boost their popularity, typically through grassroots efforts. In 2012, for example, an independent Facebook group launched a campaign that successfully voted Khan, then competing for high office, the 'Asian Person of the Year' in a poll by the Asia Society.[13]

As both countries and their politicians have expanded social-media usage, platforms such as Twitter and Facebook have become arenas for exchanging barbs. Pakistani officials, including a former national-security adviser, have repeatedly complained about India-based social-media accounts spreading disinformation about Pakistan and Afghanistan.[14] A December 2020 report by the European Union Disinformation Lab found that an anti-Pakistan narrative was being advanced by more than 750 fake media outlets and hundreds of fake accounts (including one of a deceased professor) operating in 116 countries, many of which are believed to have been coordinated by the Indian government.[15] Leaders in New Delhi have similarly blamed Pakistan for spreading anti-India disinformation on social media, pointing to a 2020 report by the Stanford University Internet Observatory that found a network of Facebook accounts being used to praise the Pakistani leadership and spread nationalist messages.[16] Both sides have used the tactic of reporting unfavourable accounts to social-media administrators and requesting that the accounts be de-activated. In short, online information campaigns have become part of the ongoing India–Pakistan conflict.

The crisis: Pulwama, Balakot and the fate of Kashmir

On 14 February 2019, a 22-year-old Kashmiri man, Adil Ahmad Dar, drove a van carrying explosives into a bus carrying members of the Indian paramilitary Central Reserve Police Force (CRPF), near the city of Pulwama. The attack killed at least 40 paramilitaries. The JeM terrorist group immediately claimed responsibility for the attack. It was the first car bomb in the region for 19 years and came after weeks of fighting that led to the deaths of eight terrorists and one Indian soldier.

The Indian government responded quickly. Two days after the attack, Indian troops targeted JeM insurgents in the Kashmiri village of Pinglan, killing three of them – including a commander, Abdul Rashi Ghazi, also known as 'Kamran' – and a civilian. Four Indian soldiers also died. In one of the stranger social-media incidents during the crisis, the international press unknowingly circulated a doctored image of Kamran that showed his face on the body of the American musician Jon Bon Jovi.[17] Indian forces would continue to attack insurgents in the region, arresting 100 separatist leaders on 23 February and engaging in a gun battle the next day that killed five.

Indian policymakers also responded on Twitter in an example of a formal narrative. On the day of the Pulwama attack, Modi tweeted:

> Attack on CRPF personnel in Pulwama is despicable. I strongly condemn this dastardly attack. The sacrifices of our brave security personnel shall not go in vain. The entire nation stands shoulder to shoulder with the families of the brave martyrs. May the injured recover quickly.[18]

Two days later, on 16 February, Modi's message escalated and promised retaliation:

> The dastardly attack in Pulwama has anguished the nation. Yes, this is a time of great sadness. But, I assure every family that a befitting reply will be given![19]

Within hours of the attack, Indian officials renounced Pakistan's most-favoured-nation status, resulting in a 200% increase in customs duties, and over the following days threatened to undermine Pakistan's economy in various ways. On 21 February, a tweet from India's minister of shipping, Nitin Gadkari, appeared to threaten to divert the Indian rivers providing some of Pakistan's water supply:

> Under the leadership of Hon'ble PM Sri @narendramodi ji, Our Govt. has decided to stop our share of water which used to flow to Pakistan. We will divert water from Eastern rivers and supply it to our people in Jammu and Kashmir and Punjab.[20]

Pakistani officials claimed India was trying to silence them on social media by reporting them to the platform administrators and requesting that their accounts be blocked because of illegal content.[21] In some cases India was successful. For example, Twitter suspended the personal account of Pakistan's foreign-ministry spokesperson, Mohammed Faisal, after a complaint by the Indian foreign ministry that he was tweeting about 'atrocities' in Kashmir while also speaking before the International Court of Justice. The account was reactivated hours later.[22]

Another notable response by the BJP on social media was to blame the rival Congress Party for failing to address the risks of terrorism, while portraying itself – and Modi in particular – as taking a firmer stance. One BJP politician argued that although the government had failed to prevent the terrorist attack, the BJP was the best hope for maintaining Indian control over Kashmir:

> BJP have failed in Kashmir and failed to properly retaliate. But BJP is capable of re-tooling itself and smash Pakistan. The opposition is in a surrender mood since long. That is the bottom line in this election. Either this possibility with BJP or give up Kashmir.[23]

The social-media activity targeting the Congress Party included various fake images and news stories. One image appeared to show the then-leader of the party, Rahul Gandhi, meeting with the terrorists. Fake videos showed Gandhi and others in his party celebrating the attacks. Meanwhile, the Congress Party accused the BJP of a counter-terrorism failure, circulating tweets critical of the handling of the crisis, and a Congress-affiliated newspaper used social media to disinter an old video of Modi, from when he was in opposition, in which he was putting a series of questions to his predecessor as prime minister, Manmohan Singh, suggesting Singh's Congress-led government was doing too little to combat terrorism – the clear message was that the same questions could now be asked of the BJP.[24]

Just days after the terrorist attack, on 17 and 19 February 2019, Saudi Crown Prince Mohammad bin Salman went to Pakistan and then India on pre-planned state visits. Saudi Arabia's then-foreign minister, Adel al-Jubeir, said his country's objective was 'to try to de-escalate tensions between [India and Pakistan], and to see if there is a path forward to resolving those differences peacefully'.[25] But it is not known if bin Salman attempted to mediate the conflict directly. If he did, India is unlikely to have welcomed the initiative, as it tends to be suspicious of third-party involvement in the issue of Kashmir.[26]

Throughout the crisis there were attacks on social media aimed at individuals – Kashmiri or otherwise – who had criticised the BJP or the Indian military. In one incident, a university professor was allegedly stalked on Facebook for voicing criticism of the Indian Army's actions in Kashmir – she subsequently resigned from her position and went into hiding.[27] Allegedly there were also calls on social media for Kashmiri students to be expelled from university, and threats to landlords that rented property to Kashmiri students, but it seems these were subsequently removed.[28] The Indian authorities denied any physical attacks on Kashmiris and claimed such reports were fake news. The CRPF tweeted:

> ADVISORY: Fake news about harassment of students from #Kashmir is being propagated by various miscreants on social media. CRPF helpline has enquired about complaints about harassment and found them incorrect. These are attempts to invoke hatred Please DO NOT circulate such posts[29]

Within a couple of days of the Pulwama attack on 16 February, a Facebook group called 'Clean the Nation' was set up with the purpose of 'cleaning and weeding out anti nationals who wear the tag of Indian but leave no stones unturned to insult and mock their own people, culture and the army that is one of the best in the world'.[30] Although the account was deleted soon afterwards, the group claimed to have been responsible for filing complaints that led to the removal of more than 50 anti-government social-media accounts; it later won a prize from a far-right organisation for its efforts, with a BJP minister in attendance at the award ceremony.[31] More generally, political violence in India has been increasingly organised through social media, particularly WhatsApp, including lynchings in response to rumours of child kidnapping or killing cows.[32]

On 26 February, after 12 days of skirmishes, India responded more forcefully with an airstrike on a JeM madrassa in Balakot, Pakistan. The first public announcement of the attack came on Twitter from Pakistan Army spokesman Major General Asif Ghafoor.[33] The Pakistani Air Force retaliated the next day when its aircraft crossed the LoC and engaged the Indian Air Force. In the resulting dogfight an Indian MiG-21 was shot down and its pilot, Abhinandan Varthaman, was captured in Azad Jammu and Kashmir by Pakistan Army soldiers just as he was about to be beaten by a mob.

Pakistani commentators, including several journalists, used social media to argue that with its airstrike on Balakot, India had clearly escalated the conflict by attacking Pakistani territory. One columnist, Mosharraf Zaidi, tweeted:

> Just to be clear: #Balakot is not in Azad Kashmir. If Indian Air Force planes dropped payload in Balakot, they crossed across the LOC, and then across the entirety of Azad Kashmir, and then into Khyber Pakhtukhwa. India didn't 'cross the LOC'. It has attacked Pakistan.[34]

Meanwhile, Indians on social media were celebrating the attack. An Indian journalist, Kanchan Gupta, tweeted:

> Because neither Jaish nor its sugar daddy #Pakistan believed it's #NewIndia? Because of limp response to 26/11 [the 2008 Mumbai attacks] they couldn't imagine #IndiaStrikesBack? Because @ImranKhanPTI thought PM @narendramodi was listening to The Beatles 'White Album' last night? Happens. #Balakot #Pulwama[35]

Gupta describes himself in his Twitter profile as a 'Senior Adviser' in India's Ministry of Information and Broadcasting, blurring the lines between a government and non-government actor.

There were two main disputes between India and Pakistan about the final days of the crisis, both of which played out on social media. India contended that it destroyed the madrassa targeted on 26 February, killing at least 300 people. Subsequent open-source intelligence, however, showed there was no damage to the building, and Pakistan claimed no one was killed in the strike. One possible explanation for India's assertion is that there had been extensive calls on social media for 'hundreds' to be killed in retaliation for the Pulwama attack, which could have shaped the government narrative.[36] If so, this would appear to be an interesting example of trying to control a narrative by making an exaggerated claim that a popular demand for punitive action had been met, without actually inflicting the sort of punishment that was being demanded by the public – and so keeping a lid on escalation.

The other dispute was over whether the Indian Air Force had destroyed a Pakistani plane. Varthaman claimed to have shot down a Pakistani F-16 before his own plane was downed, but there were no reports from the US Department of Defense, which is required to track the status of all F-16s, that one had been lost. Varthaman was released on 1 March, with competing claims as to whether this was a 'gesture for peace', as claimed by the Pakistani government, or a response to threats from India about what would happen if he were detained any longer. Modi later claimed, while campaigning for re-election, that India had told Pakistan it would retaliate with surface-to-surface missiles if the pilot was not released.[37]

These two issues illustrate the importance of narratives but also a lack of alignment between descriptions of the same event. Each government would undoubtedly have benefitted if the other had confirmed their version of the story, but their main priority was to have their narrative believed by their own people. It was important for both to show that they had stood up for their nation and had not been humiliated, and their ability to do this made it possible to de-escalate the crisis. One of the issues for a government capable of using social media to encourage a burst of nationalist fervour during a crisis is that it may subsequently need to turn it off again. India's retaliation and claims of casualties in the Balakot airstrike allowed New Delhi to satisfy domestic demands without further action, with social media helping it to spread its message, while Pakistan's claims that there were no casualties allowed it to refrain from further retaliation. De-escalation therefore depended on the two sides having competing narratives for face-saving purposes.

Following Varthaman's release on 1 March, the crisis abated. Modi's apparent demonstration of strong leadership and related anti-Pakistan sentiment had bolstered his fortunes. The BJP won the general elections held between 11 April and 23 May, with Modi securing a larger share of the vote than in the 2014 elections.[38] The situation in Kashmir worsened after the elections, however. On 5 August the Indian parliament revoked Kashmir's autonomous status and troops were deployed to the region to impose curfews. Internet access in the region was either limited or cut off entirely. India went further on 31 October by revoking Kashmir's autonomy and dividing it into two separate union territories – Jammu and Kashmir, and Ladakh – which would be ruled directly from New Delhi. Indian social-media companies were later accused of being complicit in Modi's crackdown.[39]

Digital information campaigns and crisis management in the Kashmir crisis

Given that the Indian public and policymakers use social media much more extensively than their Pakistani counterparts, this analysis of the 2019 crisis has largely focused on Indian social-media activity. Nonetheless, as indicated by the Stanford University Internet Observatory's 2020 report, Pakistan is a rising player in social-media campaigns and is using platforms such as Facebook and Instagram to spread and amplify nationalist messages, with India as the target.

During the crisis the most prominent narrative promulgated on Indian social media portrayed India as the victim of Pakistani-sponsored terrorism, and used the crisis to argue that the BJP was stronger than the Congress Party would be in countering terrorism and maintaining control of Kashmir in the lead-up to the April–May elections. More extreme versions of the narrative portrayed anyone critical of the BJP as treacherous and advocated retaliatory strikes against Pakistan. The narrative predated 2019, aligned with the pre-existing views of many BJP supporters, and was directed at the Indian public and diaspora. Most of the social-media activity should be understood in the context of the upcoming elections, rather than as an attempt by the Modi government to coerce or influence Pakistani behaviour during the crisis.

To construct and disseminate this narrative, the BJP used a combination of tactics that largely relied on volunteers rather than government actors or agents. Modi himself only tweeted about the crisis a handful of times, and most government officials were relatively quiet about it on Twitter. Instead the narrative was spread through bot-generated tweets and WhatsApp messages dispersed through the BJP's 900,000-strong volunteer network, known as the smartphone *pramukhs* ('chiefs').[40] In preparation for the 2019 elections the BJP compiled lists of supporters who had smartphones, then selected *pramukhs* who would typically create three WhatsApp groups for each polling station in their area, with up to 256 people in each group (the maximum group size on WhatsApp), and act as hubs for the distribution of campaign materials and messages.[41] The groups were mostly created to look as if they consisted of ordinary citizens without any party affiliation; their purpose has been described as 'covert propaganda'.[42] Modi's deputy Amit Shah later boasted to supporters that the BJP's use of social media was an 'unstoppable force', adding that the party was capable of 'delivering any message we want to the public – whether sweet or sour, true or fake'.[43] Therefore, while seemingly independent actors were the most vocal on social media, they were often being directed by the government and using a formal government-provided narrative.

The nationalist narrative throughout the crisis was focused on the issues at hand – the terrorist attack and the tension over Kashmir. Much of the social-media activity was directed externally against Pakistan, including WhatsApp messages with the hashtag #IndiaNeedsNuclearStrike calling for the country's destruction, and showing images, videos and tweets of Pakistanis celebrating the terrorist attack, though it is unknown if these were real or fake. But this was part of a larger narrative aimed at the domestic audience, intended to shore up the Modi government and the BJP's legitimacy in the lead-up to the elections. The BJP's messaging throughout the crisis was clearly defensive and designed to reinforce pre-existing views.

Conclusion

The main role of the BJP's digital information campaigns during the 2019 India–Pakistan crisis was to amplify nationalist messages. These were created by the Modi government but disseminated largely by volunteers or in private chat groups. Rumours and fake news, such as images of Rahul Gandhi meeting with the terrorists, further reinforced these narratives but did not have a clear independent escalatory role. Similarly, social media did not provide a unique platform, different from traditional information sources, for elite-level messaging to manage the crisis, either between Modi and the Indian public or between the Indian and Pakistani leaderships. Modi's tweet on 16 February referring to imminent retaliation could be interpreted as a deterrence signal to Pakistan, but in the wider context it was aimed more at the Indian domestic audience.

In the future, these appeals to Indian nationalism could lead to escalation in a variety of ways. One potential pathway is if social-media messages became particularly convoluted and confused across different audiences. In the context of the stability–instability paradox, Krepon observed that 'escalation control requires a careful and correct reading of one's adversary. Regrettably, problems of misperception on the subcontinent have grown as the wall of separation between India and Pakistan becomes higher and thicker.'[44] If Indian social-media messages intended for the domestic audience were interpreted by Pakistan as attempts at coercion or escalation, Islamabad might be provoked to pre-emptively escalate in the future.

Another, more likely pathway would be if Indian nationalist messages on social media increase pressure on political leaders to escalate. Jeffrey Lewis refers to a 'blowback effect' in social media whereby political leaders can become trapped in their own narrative and forced along a pathway they might otherwise have avoided.[45] Similarly, Jeffrey Michaels captured the idea of a 'discourse trap' in which language and narratives that leaders have been using come to limit the scope of their decision-making.[46] In this case, if the medium is the message, leaders in India may be constrained by what is popular and permissible in the social-media narrative. In South Asia, the BJP's social-media strategy might create not only support for the party but also a highly reactive nationalist base that could demand a harsher response the next time there is a crisis over Kashmir. In 2019, the most important role played by social media in de-escalation was in promulgating a narrative that was false and yet, because it exaggerated India's military response, gave the government political leeway to wind down the conflict. This case demonstrates the complex relationship between social-media campaigns and political effects. It is natural to assume that aggressive information campaigns reinforce aggressive actions. Yet they can also be a form of misdirection and a source of political cover, demonstrating to a domestic audience a tough attitude yet combining it with careful action, claiming, for example, against the evidence, that an adversary has backed down.

CHAPTER THREE

US–Iran, 2020

In the early hours of 3 January 2020, during a visit to Baghdad, General Qasem Soleimani of the Islamic Revolutionary Guard Corps (IRGC) was killed by a US drone. Soleimani was regularly described as the second-most powerful man in Iran, after Supreme Leader Ayatollah Ali Khamenei.[1] He headed the IRGC's Quds Force, whose unconventional-warfare activities included using force on behalf of Iran's partners in the Middle East, such as by orchestrating militia attacks against American and Israeli interests in the region. The assassination came after nearly a week of rising tensions, including the killing of a US contractor in Iraq on 27 December, an American airstrike against targets in Iraq and Syria on 30 December, and an attack on the US embassy in Baghdad by an Iraqi Shia mob on 31 December. Following Soleimani's death, American and Iranian leaders took to social media. The crisis generated hundreds of posts on Twitter and Instagram, the latter being one of the few permitted social-media platforms in Iran at the time, before it de-escalated following Iran's accidental shooting down of a Ukrainian passenger plane on 8 January.

During the crisis, American and Iranian leaders used Twitter to engage publicly with each other in unprecedented fashion. Exchanges between then-president Donald Trump and Iran's then-foreign minister Javad Zarif, for example, were not – at least on the US side – filtered through government-approved talking points or press conferences, nor passed through private channels or intermediaries. One of the most contentious tweets came from Trump on 4 January, when he threatened to destroy Iranian cultural sites if the crisis escalated. In general, however, online information campaigns did not play an independent or unique role in the escalation or de-escalation of this crisis. Even though the US and Iran do not have diplomatic relations, traditional means of communication, particularly through Switzerland as an intermediary, were more relevant to the escalation dynamics. An additional and unforeseeable factor was Iran's accidental shooting down of a Ukrainian passenger airliner. The main effect of Trump's tweets was to leave the formal American narrative garbled. Trump was appealing to his domestic base, while the foreign-policy leadership, particularly secretary of state Mike Pompeo, directed their messages more to US allies and other international actors. Iran used the crisis to reinforce its pre-existing narrative that it is a regional leader confronting American neo-imperialism.

The crisis raised thorny questions about state-led information campaigns. Most noticeably, although Trump was acting independently and his tweets were organic in nature, did they represent the views of the US government? Were they part of an agreed narrative? Trump was clearly not coordinating with other actors in the executive branch of the US government, as could be seen from the disjunction between his and Pompeo's tweets. Yet the president's tweets would naturally be interpreted as conveying the view of his administration.

This is where our analytic framework can help provide clarity: although Trump's tweets were not obviously part of his government's strategy in relation to Iran, they were indicative of his determination to establish a compelling legitimacy narrative as part of his response to continuing efforts to challenge his position internally, including impeachment proceedings. They were therefore best understood as part of a larger defensive campaign by the president to portray himself as a strong leader in comparison with his predecessors. This type of narrative is also familiar in autocracies, as will be seen later in the Russia–Ukraine case study.

The lead-up to the crisis: the Iran nuclear deal, 'maximum pressure' and internet shutdown

The US and Iran have not had diplomatic relations since 1980, following the Iranian Revolution in 1979 and the 1979–81 hostage crisis in which the US embassy in Tehran was stormed and 52 Americans were held hostage for 444 days. The relationship has remained tense ever since. During that period Washington and Tehran have often referred to each other as their primary enemy and security threat. Iran incorporated the demonisation of the US into its national narratives justifying the conservative religious regime, referring to America as the 'great Satan'.[2] And on the American side, in 2002, then-president George W. Bush depicted Iran as part of an 'axis of evil' consisting of regimes seeking weapons of mass destruction. Every subsequent occupant of the White House has also described Iran as a regional menace.

Iran's nuclear ambitions are a priority concern for the US. Intelligence reports throughout the early 2000s provided evidence of Iran's growing nuclear programme and led to a series of crippling sanctions by the US and other states. Following numerous failed attempts at dialogue, a breakthrough came in 2013 with talks between Iran and the five permanent members of the UN Security Council (China, France, Russia, the UK and the US) and Germany, collectively known as the P5+1. Additionally, the US and Iran engaged in secret bilateral talks in Oman. After years of negotiations the talks resulted in the Joint Comprehensive Plan of Action (JCPOA), whereby Iran agreed to limit its enrichment activities in exchange for conditional sanctions relief.

There is some debate as to whether social media facilitated negotiation of the JCPOA. Zarif, Iran's foreign minister from 2013–21, had joined Twitter in 2009 and was active there throughout the negotiations. On 28 March 2015, for example, he tweeted:

> In negotiations, both sides must show flexibility. We have, and are ready to make a good deal for all. We await our counterparts' readiness.[3]

The Australian analyst Constance Duncombe has argued that Twitter allowed for more informal and continuous communication between Zarif and his US counterpart, secretary of state John Kerry: 'Iranian Twitter posts in the lead-up to the 2015 nuclear deal helped Iran to indicate its intention to work towards a positive outcome, an intention that was key to the successful implementation of the Joint Comprehensive Plan of Action.'[4] According to Duncombe, the above tweet from Zarif indicated an interest in cooperation and helped build trust towards dialogue. Twitter provided an alternative line of communication, which arguably was particularly important given the lack of formal diplomatic relations. Yet Wendy Sherman, the JCPOA lead negotiator, stressed the importance of Kerry's approach to building personal relationships. Twitter was not mentioned in her account of the negotiations.[5] So although these formal tweets by Kerry and Zarif might have been helpful in reinforcing messages delivered by other, more traditional means, it seems they were not especially significant – and indeed perhaps had less importance than the communication that took place at press conferences, when meanings can be clarified, and through the established 'diplomatic channels', when it might be possible to be more explicit and direct. Their main significance may have been as a signal of Iranian intent to a wider audience, but there is no evidence that on their own they advanced the negotiations.

Iran and the P5+1 proceeded with implementing the terms of the deal in the three years that followed, but on 8 May 2018 Trump withdrew the US from the agreement.[6] His administration justified withdrawal on the grounds that Iran had negotiated in bad faith, and that the JCPOA was a bad deal because it did not address Iran's missile programme and 'foolishly gave the Iranian regime a windfall of cash and access to the international financial system for trade and investment'.[7] American withdrawal from the JCPOA was part of the Trump administration's campaign of 'maximum pressure', to which Iran often responded with its own escalatory measures. Whereas Iran could not respond in kind economically to maximum pressure, it could respond militarily.[8] On 20 June 2019, Iran shot down an American RF-4A *Global Hawk* drone over the Strait of Hormuz.[9]

This was just one of many incidents that contributed to growing tensions in 2019. In early July the UK seized an Iranian oil tanker in Gibraltar, bound for Syria in violation of international sanctions.[10] Two weeks later Iran seized British-flagged oil tankers in the Strait of Hormuz (they were released in September).[11] In October Iran claimed that two missiles had struck one of its oil tankers off the coast of Saudi Arabia.[12]

Meanwhile Israel continued its 'shadow war' on Iran, target-ing cargo ships and attacking bases in Syria.[13] The analyst Ali Vaez of the International Crisis Group argued at the time that 'we're still in an escalatory spiral that risks getting out of control'.[14] In the latter half of 2019 Iran exceeded the JCPOA limits on uranium enrichment and restarted enrichment at its Fordow plant.

Although Iran was determined to show no sign that it was submitting to the maximum-pressure campaign, weaknesses were becoming evident. The economic situation created an internal crisis. Following a cutback in gasoline subsidies, mass protests erupted in Tehran and prompted a government crackdown in November 2019, during which police report-edly killed 1,500 unarmed protesters.[15] The regime took steps to limit opposition from outside and within, including by cutting internet access to just 5–7% of normal connectivity.[16] The Atlantic Council assessed that this was the largest internet shutdown in history in terms of its scale and effec-tiveness.[17] It was even more drastic than the government's response to the Green Movement in 2009 following that year's contested presidential elections, when internet access was severely restricted.[18]

The 2009 and 2019 protests were also turning points in the Iranian regime's control of social media. In the wake of the Green Movement it passed new laws to regulate social-media usage and created new entities to enforce them. Between 2012 and 2016 it shut down the majority of social-media sites, including Facebook and Twitter. Instagram and Telegram, a Russian-owned app, were the most popular of the remaining platforms, with 24m and 40m users respectively.[19] During this time the regime also developed its approach to information warfare, including social media. Throughout the 2010s, accord-ing to the Atlantic Council, Iran's digital influence operations represented 'a continuation of public diplomacy', targeted at domestic audiences but also potentially favourable international ones, to which Iran presented itself as a force against Western neo-colonialism. The regime used social media and other digital tools to promote this narrative.[20] Iran began using 'sock puppets' – fake accounts employed to amplify and spread messages on social media – as early as 2010, and launched 'cyber battalions' and bots from 2011.[21] By the time of the 2019 protests and 2020 crisis, Iran had a well-developed digital strategy with various tools at its disposal.

The crisis: Soleimani's assassination, Switzerland as messenger and de-escalation

On 27 December 2019, an Iraqi pro-Iranian Shia militia, Kataib Hizbullah, killed a US contractor in Kirkuk in a rocket attack on a US military base. It was the tenth missile attack connected to the Iranian-backed militia in two months.[22] On 29 December the US retaliated with an airstrike on the militia, killing 25 and wounding 50. Trump took to Twitter to announce the American response:

> Iran killed an American contractor, wounding many. We strongly responded, and always will. Now Iran is orchestrating an attack on the U.S. Embassy in Iraq. They will be held fully responsible. In addition, we expect Iraq to use its forces to protect the Embassy, and so notified! … Iran will be held fully responsible for lives lost, or damage incurred, at any of our facilities. They will pay a very BIG PRICE! This is not a Warning, it is a Threat. Happy New Year![23]

Trump also repeatedly retweeted Senator Lindsey Graham, who had said 'he [Trump] has put the world on notice. There will be no Benghazis on his watch.'[24] This was a reference to the attacks on the diplomatic compound and other US facilities in Benghazi, Libya, in 2012, in which the US ambassador was assassinated – the incident had led Republicans to question the competence and integrity of then-secretary of state Hillary Clinton. Although Trump's tweet could be interpreted as a signal to deter any Iranian response, it also had a domestic audience. His tweets were typically intended to appeal to his electoral base. His impeachment trial was set to begin just two weeks later, on 16 January 2020.

In response to the American airstrike, a mob led by members of Kataib Hizbullah, among others, attacked the US embassy in Baghdad, but with no reported casualties. Then-secretary of defense Mark Esper announced on Twitter that the US would deploy the Immediate Response Force to the region. Hours later, Ayatollah Khamenei used Twitter to threaten the US:

> If the Islamic Republic decides to challenge & fight, it will do so unequivocally. We're not after wars, but we strongly defend the Iranian nation's interests, dignity, & glory. If anyone threatens that, we will unhesitatingly confront & strike them.[25]

Again, this could be interpreted as a deterrence signal, but if so, it failed to prevent American action. President Trump was reportedly presented with several different options for responding to the embassy attack, with the killing of Soleimani assessed by military and civilian advisers to be the most extreme.[26] Trump had previously considered assassinating Soleimani but had rejected the option on the advice of his inner circle because of potential escalatory effects.[27] This time, however, he chose to strike.

Soleimani had flown from Syria to Baghdad on a passenger plane at the invitation of the Iraqi government, arriving in the early hours of 3 January. No obvious precautions had been taken to conceal his travel plans.[28] The US drone strike took place as he was leaving the airport, killing him and also Kataib Hizbullah's Iraqi leader, Abu Mahdi al-Muhandis. The US had planned to assassinate a leader of the Quds Force in Yemen at the same time, but the operation failed due to poor intelligence. American officials did not notify any allies in advance of the attack, although Pompeo apparently hinted at it in a conversation with Israeli Prime Minister Benjamin Netanyahu the day before.[29] At the time of his death, Soleimani was a popular figure in Iran and his online profile was gaining traction. This was due partly to social media, for example the circulation of selfies and other images of him alongside Iranian-backed militias in Iraq. His funeral was reportedly attended by millions of Iranians.[30]

Immediately after the drone strike and in the following days, the US and Iran communicated through diplomatic channels. Via the Swiss embassy in Tehran, which acted as an intermediary, the US sent messages urging Iran not to escalate. Switzerland had served as a neutral actor between the US and Iran since the end of diplomatic relations in 1980, attempting to resolve conflicts and bring the two sides to the negotiating table.[31] It had initiated the talks that culminated in the JCPOA and facilitated a prisoner exchange in 2019. According to Iran's deputy foreign minister Mohsen Baharvand, in an interview with the Iranian state-run Fars News Agency, the US message received via the Swiss ambassador 'was rejected immediately'.[32]

The American and Iranian leaders also took to social media as they attempted to shape the narrative around the growing crisis. On the US side, Trump sent a tweet that emphasised

Soleimani's role in attacks against Americans in the Middle East, portraying him as a thug who had been allowed to operate freely for years before finally being brought to justice:

> General Qassem Soleimani has killed or badly wounded thousands of Americans over an extended period of time, and was plotting to kill many more... but got caught! He was directly and indirectly responsible for the death of millions of people, including the recent large number.... .....of PROTESTERS killed in Iran itself. While Iran will never be able to properly admit it, Soleimani was both hated and feared within the country. They are not nearly as saddened as the leaders will let the outside world believe. He should have been taken out many years ago![33]

While Trump used Twitter to justify the US action, Iran's leadership used it to try to shape the international narrative about the US. Twitter was banned in Iran (and still is, although Iranians continue to access it via VPN and other workarounds), so presumably much of Tehran's messaging was directed towards an international audience. A tweet from then-foreign minister Zarif, for example, pinned the blame for any escalation on the US and 'its rogue adventurism'.[34]

The Twitter exchange took a dramatic turn on 4 January when Trump threatened to target Iranian cultural sites if the conflict escalated:

> Iran is talking very boldly about targeting certain USA assets as revenge for our ridding the world of their terrorist leader who had just killed an American, & badly wounded many others, not to mention all of the people he had killed over his lifetime, including

recently.... ....hundreds of Iranian protesters. He was already attacking our Embassy, and preparing for additional hits in other locations. Iran has been nothing but problems for many years. Let this serve as a WARNING that if Iran strikes any Americans, or American assets, we have.... ....targeted 52 Iranian sites (representing the 52 American hostages taken by Iran many years ago), some at a very high level & important to Iran & the Iranian culture, and those targets, and Iran itself, WILL BE HIT VERY FAST AND VERY HARD. The USA wants no more threats![35]

The following day, Iran announced it would no longer restrict its uranium enrichment and asked for a meeting with the Swiss ambassador.[36]

Over the next three days, US leaders sent mixed messages both through traditional diplomatic channels and via Twitter. Trump continued to threaten Iran, and at one point retweeted a comment suggesting his was a clever deterrence strategy with a clear red line.[37] But others within the US administration took steps to de-escalate the situation. Pompeo attempted to balance Trump's tweets with one of his own, expressing respect for Persian culture:

> The United States was founded on tolerance. We have great respect for Persian history and its symbols, like Persepolis, Naqsh-e Jahan Square, and the Tomb of Cyrus. @khamenei_ir's corrupt regime should listen to the people of #Iran. They want their culture and their country back.[38]

Trump's messaging did not follow the normal internal processes within the US government, and it is unclear whether these messages were developed by his staff with input from the relevant agencies. There had already been a number of cases in which Trump had apparently made policy announcements on Twitter but then there had been very little follow-up, as it transpired that those tweets had done no more than express an intention. Therefore, either in the US or elsewhere, those familiar with Trump's Twitter activity would not necessarily have assumed that his tweets during the crisis were indicators of forthcoming action, unless their validity was confirmed by statements from other key officials.

On 7 January, Pompeo sent a series of tweets referring to calls with regional allies in which he had stressed that the US 'does not seek war and is committed to de-escalation'.[39] At the time, Iran was hosting the Tehran Dialogue Forum, attended by hundreds of officials and other participants from around the region. One of them, the foreign minister of Oman, delivered a message to the Iranian leadership from Washington, expressing a desire to de-escalate the situation.[40] Although Trump's stance, including his tweets, complicated the diplomacy and introduced an extra degree of uncertainty, the crisis was being managed through more traditional diplomatic means, away from public platforms.

Later that day, 7 January, Iran retaliated by firing more than a dozen ballistic missiles at two Iraqi bases hosting US troops. As a political message the attack was significant: it came directly from Iran itself, not from proxy forces, and was admitted by Tehran. Although no Americans were killed, it was unclear whether this was intentional. If intentional, it could be considered a case of honour satisfied without escalation. It seems the US base commanders had advance warning of the attack, which would have allowed the troops to take shelter beforehand.[41]

Shortly after the attack, Zarif declared on Twitter that it was justified on grounds of self-defence:

Iran took & concluded proportionate measures in self-defense under Article 51 of UN Charter targeting base from which cowardly armed attack against our citizens & senior officials were launched. We do not seek escalation or war, but will defend ourselves against any aggression.[42]

On Instagram, Ayatollah Khamenei sent a very undiplomatic message: an image of Trump with a red handprint on his face, with the fingers in the shape of missiles, accompanied by the caption 'just a slap, revenge is another matter'.[43] Appearing to ignore this personal attack, Trump tweeted shortly afterwards:

All is well! Missiles launched from Iran at two military bases located in Iraq. Assessment of casualties & damages taking place now. So far, so good! We have the most powerful and well equipped military anywhere in the world, by far! I will be making a statement tomorrow morning.[44]

The IRGC's deputy commander, Ali Fadavi, would later claim on Iranian state television that Washington had essentially told Tehran, through the Swiss, 'if you want to get revenge, get revenge in proportion to what we did'. The US government disputes this, however.[45] Trump's 'All is well!' tweet and subsequent reassurances by Esper and Pompeo, both on social media and through diplomatic channels, suggested the US was not going to retaliate following the missile strikes and that the crisis was abating.

Just as Trump was sending his 'All is well!' tweet, Iran accidentally shot down a Ukrainian Airlines passenger jet, killing 176 passengers and crew. The last flight data was received at 6.14am Tehran time on 8 January (9.44pm on 7 January, US East

Coast time); Trump's tweet was sent at 9.45pm EST.[46] The incident was the result of heightened alert within Iran due to the crisis. On 11 January, after three days of official denials and increasing public pressure, Zarif acknowledged the accident:

> A sad day. Preliminary conclusions of internal investigation by Armed Forces: Human error at time of crisis caused by US adventurism led to disaster. Our profound regrets, apologies and condolences to our people, to the families of all victims, and to other affected nations.[47]

The crisis noticeably eased after this. Trump barely mentioned it on Twitter, with his attention shifting to the impeachment trial. And Iran was deeply embarrassed not only by the shooting down of the aircraft but also by its inability to protect a top general at the outset of the crisis.[48]

The broader US–Iran relationship remained tense, however. Pompeo announced on Twitter that Washington would continue its policy of maximum pressure, including new sanctions. In November 2020 a leading Iranian nuclear scientist was killed by an Israeli agent, and the International Atomic Energy Agency reported that Iran's uranium stockpiles exceeded JCPOA limits – its centrifuges in Natanz were now active and there were some inconsistencies in Iran's reporting. In 2021, with Trump replaced in the White House by Joe Biden, talks between the parties to the JCPOA took place in Vienna, but ultimately diplomatic attempts to renegotiate a nuclear deal stalled. A major sticking point was the Iranian demand that the IRGC be removed from the US terror blacklist. In June 2022 the US announced a new round of sanctions against Iran's oil industry, and relations between the two countries have also been negatively affected by Iranian military support for Russia's invasion of Ukraine.

Digital information campaigns and crisis management in the US–Iran relationship

The US and Iran both used digital information campaigns to advance their respective narratives during the 2020 crisis. The way the US did so raises the question of who determines a national narrative during a crisis, particularly when events are unfolding quickly. Contrasting tweets by senior US officials demonstrated that the US narrative was inconsistent and probably uncoordinated. Trump used Twitter to advance a nationalist narrative to domestic audiences, portraying the US as a victim of ongoing Iranian terrorism and aggression in the Middle East. This was a defensive narrative that largely aligned with many Americans' pre-existing views about Iran and focused on the issue at hand.

But Trump also used Twitter to advance another narrative, which attempted to justify an aggressive response to Iran and asserted his personal qualities as a dealmaker and promoter of US national security. Trump's tweets repeatedly criticised the Obama administration's handling of Iran, particularly its negotiation of the JCPOA, and used the crisis to amplify his message. For example, on 7 January, Trump retweeted a tweet from Republican National Committee Chairwoman Ronna McDaniel, praising him in comparison to Obama:

> How terrible was the Obama-Biden Iran policy? In 2016, their Secretary of State John Kerry admitted that some Iranian sanctions relief money would fund terrorism. @realDonaldTrump is cleaning up their mess![49]

This tweet also linked to a CNN article with the headline 'John Kerry: Some Sanctions Relief Money for Iran Will Go to Terrorism'.[50] Trump retweeted similar messages from senators Lindsay Graham and Marco Rubio.[51] In this case, as in many others, he turned the narrative about the crisis into a narrative about himself.

The Iranian regime's social-media activity during the crisis deliberately amplified its pre-existing narrative of resistance to American neo-colonialism and imperialism. The regime restricts the Iranian public's access to the internet and social media, and despite the workarounds through which some Iranians are able to access Twitter, it is reasonable to assume the tweets from Iranian officials quoted in this chapter were largely intended for an international audience. According to research by the Atlantic Council, the Iranian regime's social-media activity during the crisis largely focused on the American political leadership, with calls for violent retaliation that included an image posted on Instagram of Trump's decapitated head.[52] Another widely shared image, sent to numerous White House officials, showed coffins draped in American flags. Since the crisis, Tehran has continued to use social media to spread disinformation in an attempt to undermine Western narratives and democratic governments. It was particularly active in spreading conspiracy theories about the origins of COVID-19 and trying to undermine American vaccination programmes.[53]

The US–Iran case also illustrates broader trends in crisis escalation. There are essentially two views of escalation. The first is that it is a tragic dynamic, a consequence of the main actors losing control of a process and reacting in panic to a rumour or to a move they fear their adversary will make. The other is that it is a deliberate, strategic move designed to obtain a more advantageous situation. It can, of course, be a combination of the two, with policymakers weighing the interests at stake, and the competing risks of action and inaction, while also reacting more impulsively to domestic and international political pressures. This US–Iran crisis appears to have been an example of such a combination.

Many other factors and actors were involved as the crisis escalated and may have had an important impact on its outcome: Switzerland playing the role of intermediary; Oman passing on peace messages during the Tehran Dialogue Forum; and also an unexpected event – the shooting down of the Ukrainian airliner. An official in the Trump administration would later point to the importance of Switzerland's mediation: 'When tensions with Iran were high, the Swiss played a useful and reliable role that both sides appreciated. Their system is like a light that never turns off. We don't communicate with the Iranians that much, but when we do the Swiss have played a critical role to convey messages and avoid miscalculation.'[54]

Conclusion

We can envision at least two ways the crisis could have taken a different turn and been negatively affected by the dynamics of social media. Firstly, our analysis has assumed that Iran intended its retaliatory missile strikes on US forces in Iraq to be proportionate and cause minimal loss of life, given that it seems US troops had sufficient advance warning to enable them to take cover. If Iran had in fact caused a significant loss of US lives, especially following Trump's Twitter bombast, social media would probably have amplified calls among US domestic audiences for military retaliation and further escalation. At this point Trump and other US decision-makers might have found themselves boxed in and obliged to respond to the pressure. A second way the crisis could have escalated was if another US official had adopted a tone and narrative similar to Trump's. If Esper had approved and affirmed Trump's threat to target cultural sites, for example, that might have provoked a more aggressive response from Iran.

In the event, however, Trump's tweets were just one form of overt communication during the crisis, and not the most important. By this stage in his presidency many of his tweets and public statements were being treated with a degree of circumspection. He appeared to be misaligned with his own government, so his comments were less likely to be taken seriously. Furthermore, although in other case studies we describe the significant impact of governments' digital information campaigns on domestic audiences, it is worth noting that in this crisis it was not the case. Trump was seeking a boost ahead of his upcoming impeachment trial and the November 2020 election, but the crisis was over too quickly to have a major positive impact on his popularity. And in Iran, given the public's limited access to social media, it seems likely that many of the regime's messages on those platforms, particularly Twitter, were geared more to international than to domestic opinion. Those messages seem not to have had a significant impact abroad, however, as there were no major shifts in Iran's alliances or adversaries during or after the crisis.

CHAPTER FOUR

China and the COVID-19 pandemic, 2020–22

In early 2020 there were reports of a deadly new virus in China, which soon began to spread to other parts of the world. The World Health Organization (WHO) declared COVID-19 to be a pandemic on 11 March, by which time many countries had already adopted a range of emergency measures, from travel bans to full lockdowns. In the months that followed, governments grappled with the social, political and economic consequences of the pandemic while seeking to develop vaccines and new treatments.

Forced to spend much longer at home than usual, people around the world increasingly went online and turned to social media for information. According to one study, Americans' average time spent on social media increased from 54 to 65 minutes per day during 2020; other studies put the figure even higher.[1] Social media became important not only as a means by which people could connect, but also for information about vaccines, international travel and government programmes to combat the pandemic. Lives were spent online to a greater extent than before. While the pandemic was not a military crisis like those in the other case studies in this volume, the ways in which governments handled it – and the related digital information campaigns – demonstrated trends in digital narratives that are of wider relevance to crisis management. For example, the delays and obfuscations in China's early response to COVID-19, the WHO's early statements in support of China, and Beijing's reluctance to have its response investigated led China to develop and refine its approach to digital information campaigns.

China came late to the social-media game compared to Russia and Iran, but it became a major player during the pandemic. Beijing developed strategies for information campaigns to control the narrative, particularly at home, while also undermining Western narratives about COVID-19. A 2021 study by the Atlantic Council and Associated Press, for example, found that China was becoming a leader in disinformation.[2] Its activities expanded well beyond maintaining the Great Firewall. It continued to evolve its tactics so as to build an ever-wider network for disseminating false narratives and reinforcing pre-existing claims. This network has grown to include not only sock puppets (fake accounts) and 'astroturfing' (giving the impression of a grassroots campaign), but also the use of influencers and Chinese officials, along with established television and print-media networks, to spread disinformation.[3] The role of Chinese diplomats as 'wolf warriors', taking an assertive and combative stance whenever China's reputation was perceived to be slighted, demonstrated its readiness to take positions that played well at home, and could reinforce nationalist feeling, though they played badly abroad.[4]

The lead-up to the crisis: China's growing social-media presence

Beijing's online disinformation efforts became increasingly apparent in 2014. A RAND Corporation report on China's social-media activities points to fake Twitter accounts at that time which circulated positive messages about China's rule of Tibet during a period of unrest in the region.[5] China's social-media activities expanded in 2015 with the establishment of the People's Liberation Army (PLA) Strategic Support Force as a separate service with a focus on information warfare.[6] Many of the early examples of digital disinformation appeared to be focused on controlling domestic opinion or on blurring the international audience's view of Chinese issues.[7]

In 2016 Beijing launched a digital campaign to spread disinformation in the lead-up to the Taiwan presidential elections. It also spammed the Facebook account of the frontrunner and eventual winner, Tsai Ing-Wen, with tens of thousands of posts demanding that Taiwan and mainland China be reunified.[8] Taiwan has remained a focus of China's information operations ever since. In the 2018 local elections there, China again disseminated anti-Tsai propaganda on numerous social-media platforms, including Twitter, which was then picked up by legitimate news sources and widely disseminated.[9] The 2018 interference was so extreme that it prompted a bipartisan group of six US senators – three Democrats and three Republicans – to write a letter accusing the Chinese Communist Party (CCP) of 'using disinformation to shape public opinion of political candidates deemed unsympathetic to Beijing's interests'.[10]

None of this harmed Tsai Ing-Wen. She was re-elected in 2020 despite another period of extensive social-media activity by Beijing aimed at influencing the election outcome. A group of YouTube users in Taiwan identified 59 channels responsible for spreading a pro-Beijing narrative promoting reunification; some of them had tens of thousands of subscribers and millions of views. While there was no explicit link between these channels and the CCP, they had similar layouts and messaging that resembled those of the government in Beijing.[11] China's social-media activities in Taiwan sought not only to undermine anti-Beijing politicians but also to promote a more favourable image of China in the hope of making reunification more appealing. Taiwan seems to have served as a test bed for developing increasingly sophisticated disinformation messages and networks, which China then deployed elsewhere.[12] There is no evidence, however, that this made much difference to public opinion in Taiwan, which has remained broadly negative towards Beijing.[13]

Aside from Taiwan, the Chinese government employed information campaigns during the 2019 protests in Hong Kong in opposition to an extradition bill imposed by Beijing. During the protests Beijing widely disseminated disinformation through fake accounts promoting the largely false narrative that the protesters were violent. China's activities led to decisions by Facebook and Twitter in August 2019 to suspend thousands of accounts. Twitter found 900 accounts 'deliberately and specifically attempting to sow political discord in Hong Kong', including a network of linked accounts aimed at amplifying the Beijing government's messages.[14] According to Twitter, 'based on our intensive investigations, we have reliable evidence to support that this is a coordinated state-backed operation. Specifically, we identified large clusters of accounts behaving in a coordinated manner to amplify messages related to the Hong Kong protests.'[15] The protesters also made use of social media, with more than 100 groups on Telegram and other sites sharing information and advice in an attempt to evade the authorities in Beijing.[16] The opposition's use of social media in Hong Kong was much more effective in terms of gaining popular support, as measured for example in the results of the 2019 elections. Beijing ultimately settled the matter by cracking down on dissent during the pandemic and imposing censorship, including controls on social media, so that Hong Kong increasingly resembled an authoritarian mainland city.

During the 2010s, leaders in Beijing developed what the RAND report describes as 'cognitive domain operations', including psychological warfare and tactics designed to shape audience perception.[17] While its online tactics in the Hong Kong protests indicated new disinformation pathways, China's activity remained relatively under-developed compared to Russia's. According to one study, China's use of social media during the protests was a 'blunt-force influence operation' using fake accounts and an 'influence-for-hire network'.[18] The majority of posts were in Mandarin and Cantonese, suggesting they were targeted primarily at domestic audiences along with influential networks among the Chinese diaspora overseas. Until recently the CCP was careful to maintain a degree of plausible deniability around its social-media disinformation activities, but that changed with the arrival of COVID-19.[19]

This reflected Beijing's growing conviction, as an authoritarian government, that it was able to control social-media access even while using those platforms to amplify and intensify its chosen narratives. Online surveillance tools allow states to monitor or block certain messages and create 'digital dictatorships'.[20] As it had blocked most international social-media platforms using the Great Firewall, and closely monitored domestic platforms such as WeChat, the Chinese government was in a position to exercise a significant degree of control over the information about COVID-19 that the population received online. Externally, Beijing used international platforms to spread messages and stories that supported its handling of the pandemic while amplifying conspiracy theories about the virus having originated in the US armed forces. The number of government-affiliated social-media accounts noticeably increased during the pandemic, indicating that China was exploring how best to use social media as part of its wolf-warrior diplomacy and to promote a more favourable view of China abroad. To spread the message about Western failures and alleged Chinese success, Beijing relied on a combination of tactics – including bot networks, as reported by Bellingcat. It also used legitimate accounts, such as those of Chinese diplomats and celebrities, to spread false narratives, and encouraged astroturfing to give the impression of regional and on-the-ground movements.[21]

China's information campaigns during the pandemic drew increasingly on Russia's disinformation and social-media playbook, with the use of bots just one example.[22] Unlike Russia, however, China initially made significant efforts to conceal some of its disinformation efforts on social media, not only because of its desire to be seen as a credible great power but also seemingly because it was aware its message would probably be less well received internationally if it was obviously coming from the CCP.[23] To achieve this, one common Chinese tactic was – and still is – 'spamouflage', or flooding the information space with fake news from a bevy of accounts, some real and some not. According to Graphika, a company that specialises in the study of online communities, while social-media companies have repeatedly taken down such accounts, the networks and accounts 'have continued to revive themselves'.[24] But the pandemic complicated China's strategy of plausible deniability and drove Beijing to adopt more aggressive tactics and focus on promoting disinformation rather than suppressing critical content.[25]

At the start of the pandemic, the UN warned of a parallel 'global infodemic'.[26] Authoritarian regimes such as China, Iran and Russia had an interest in undermining US credibility and, in the words of Lauren Rosenberger and John Garnaut, 'the legitimacy of liberal democratic systems and governments, as a means of shoring up their own illiberal ones'.[27] They proved to be particularly active in spreading disinformation about the origins of the virus, and China's collusion with other opportunistic disinformation actors, particularly Russia and Iran, also helped amplify its own narrative.

The speed intrinsic to social media allows for immediate and constant messaging, and in China's case, according to the RAND study, it enabled the government to use data analytics to 'improve its messaging feedback loop for better content by revealing the content that audiences engage with'.[28] The RAND study also stated that 'PLA authors generally describe social media as a dream-come-true platform for next-generation messaging with content tailored for specific audiences', although 'there are few indications so far that the PLA has conclusively determined the role of social media in its military strategy'.[29] This means that while China recognises the potential value of social media for wolf-warrior diplomacy and reaching international audiences, it is still unsure how best to utilise these platforms and is in a learning stage, similar to Russia at the start of the Ukraine crisis (discussed in the next chapter) when it tested various narratives across multiple platforms to see which gained the most traction.

The crisis: COVID-19 outbreak, pandemic and Chinese efforts to control the narrative

In late December 2019 the Chinese government became aware of an illness spreading through the city of Wuhan.[30] It very quickly began to censor any mention of the virus on WeChat, a domestic social-media platform, but on 20 January 2020 it suddenly announced that battling COVID-19 was a 'top priority' and Xi Jinping ordered 'resolute efforts' to stop its spread. On 23 January the government closed the borders of Hubei province, of which Wuhan is the capital. On 31 January the Trump administration banned visitors from China from entering the US. The previous day, 30 January, the director-general of the WHO, Tedros Adhanom Ghebreyesus, had visited Beijing and declared a 'Public Health Emergency of International Concern', but also stated that 'the Chinese government is to be congratulated for the extraordinary measures it has taken to contain the outbreak'. He followed this up with a message on Twitter:

> In many ways, #China is actually setting a new standard for outbreak response. Our greatest concern is the potential for the virus to spread to countries with weaker health systems, and which are ill-prepared to deal with it. #2019nCoV.[31]

Claims that the disease originated in US bioweapons activity appeared soon after the outbreak began and were initially amplified by Russian state media.[32] By the end of January the main pieces were already in place for China's subsequent social-media campaign to shape the narrative around the pandemic. In mid-February, Chinese government officials and social-media accounts became noticeably more active. On 22 February the CCP newspaper the *People's Daily* published a story speculating that COVID-19 had originated in the US armed forces, and on 9 March a WeChat user posted an essay claiming not only that it had been created by the US military but also that it had been released at the Military World Games held in Wuhan in October 2019. Chinese diplomats were suddenly more visible on social media, sharing claims about the origins of the virus. The monthly total of messages sent from Chinese diplomats' Twitter accounts tripled between January 2020 and January 2021, from roughly 5,000 to 15,000.[33] The number of government-linked Twitter accounts increased from 58 to 76 between January 2019 and December 2020.[34] Activity on these accounts noticeably increased in tandem with surges in the pandemic; it peaked in March 2020, when almost 25,000 tweets from government-affiliated accounts praised or defended Beijing's response.[35]

As governments across the world struggled to contain COVID-19, Beijing stepped up its efforts to counteract the potentially negative consequences for China's image. In April, ProPublica uncovered a Twitter network leading an influence campaign with ties to the Chinese government.[36] In May, Bellingcat uncovered a bot network targeting a Chinese dissident, Miles Guo (also known as Miles Kwok), which was subsequently used to spread COVID-19 disinformation and amplify messages disparaging the US.[37] As the virus spread, so did disinformation.

Throughout the pandemic the CCP's social-media activity focused on four main narratives. First and foremost it aimed to maintain a positive image of China both domestically and on the international stage, primarily for defensive purposes to reinforce existing formal narratives coming out of Beijing. It portrayed itself as a global leader in the fight against the pandemic, frequently quoting the comments the WHO director-general had made in Beijing in late January 2020. The government was also energetic in advertising the fact that in the spring of 2020 it had donated medical-grade face masks to several European countries; this was often incorporated into messages glorifying the Chinese medical and political system and criticising Western democratic responses.[38] The European External Action Service tracked disinformation through the pandemic, reporting in May 2021:

> The efforts of state actors like China to deflect blame, to use the pandemic to promote their own governmental system and enhance their image abroad continue.

The claim that there are clandestine US biological laboratories on the territory of 'former Soviet republics' has been spread both by pro-Kremlin outlets as well as Chinese officials and state media. … China – 'having made sacrifices to buy time for the rest of the world' – is portrayed as a responsible and transparent actor in the pandemic and a model for other countries to follow. In parallel, where established facts or prevailing narratives could be seen as unfavourable to China or could support criticism of Chinese authorities there seems to be the effort of creating doubt in relation to those. For example, creating doubts about China's role in the COVID-19 outbreak and countering international calls for an independent inquiry into the origins of the outbreak of the virus in China.[39]

Perhaps one of the strangest examples of this first narrative was China's targeting of Italy. The Italian news organisation Formiche found a coordinated network of bots on Italian social-media platforms, amplifying messages coming from Chinese diplomats and undermining the European Union's response to the pandemic.[40] In the spring of 2020 a video circulated on social media apparently showing Italians singing the Chinese national anthem from their balconies, in thanks for China's medical supplies and assistance during the early stages of the pandemic. It was later proved that the video had been altered – the Italians were actually singing their own national anthem.[41] In summary, China used social media to spread the narrative that it had effectively bought time for the rest of the world through its quick response to COVID-19 and had then provided crucial assistance to Western democracies that lacked the resources to respond effectively themselves. This narrative was intended to undermine or drown out accusations about

China's handling of the initial outbreak and its possible responsibility for the pandemic.

The second narrative advanced by China on social media was that COVID-19 originated in the US armed forces. An Associated Press investigation of state-sponsored disinformation, conducted in collaboration with the Atlantic Council's Digital Forensic Research Lab, shows how this rumour was weaponised by the Chinese government and spread globally, feeding off dozens of platforms using fake and real accounts.[42] A Chinese foreign-ministry spokesperson, Zhao Lijian, sent a series of 11 aggressive tweets on 12–13 March 2020 supporting this claim and calling for American transparency, which over the next six weeks was cited almost 100,000 times (and in 54 languages) by Twitter accounts with a total of almost 275m followers.[43] As the pandemic progressed, and international pressure mounted on China to allow a WHO inspection to investigate the possible origins of the virus, Beijing attempted to deflect the pressure further onto the US. On 18 January 2021, at a press conference, the Chinese government spokesperson Hua Chunying said, 'I'd like to stress that if the United States truly respects facts, it should open the biological lab at Fort Detrick, give more transparency to issues like its 200-plus overseas bio-labs, invite WHO experts to conduct origin-tracing in the United States'.[44] China was not alone in advancing this narrative. After its initial appearance in a Russian news source, the Russian disinformation apparatus, including bots and trolls, continued to propagate the narrative that the US had secret bioweapons labs in former Soviet states, particularly Ukraine. The Iranian regime's social-media campaigns also propagated the story, retweeting the claims as early as 23 March 2020.[45]

The third narrative was a larger offensive strategy intended to undermine American credibility. China saw the pandemic as an opportunity to point to shortcomings in the American system of government, particularly under the Trump administration. In an early attempt to undermine the US response to the pandemic, in mid-March 2020 the Chinese foreign ministry used different platforms, including social media and text messages, to circulate the information that Trump was about to decree a nationwide lockdown that would be enforced by the armed forces.[46] One message read: 'They will announce this as soon as they have troops in place to help prevent looters and rioters.'[47] According to US officials, the Chinese state did not actually create these messages but amplified them across multiple platforms.[48] This tactic would prove to be a favourite of China (and Russia) on social media. Chinese state accounts, including those of diplomats, would disseminate disinformation, whether from traditional media sources or elsewhere on social media, to expand its audience by orders of magnitude.

In the fourth narrative, China undermined international medical responses to COVID-19 in various ways. In the early stages of the pandemic Beijing interfered with the publication of medical research, delaying information-sharing about the effects of the virus.[49] Later it spread disinformation on the efficacy and safety of the Western COVID-19 vaccines that formed the basis of Washington's 'vaccine diplomacy' strategy. This is one example of an offensive information campaign intended to shift audience views. For China, challenging Western vaccines served the greater purpose of undermining trust in European and American institutions.[50] The Chinese state-controlled media spread stories about political disputes over vaccines to highlight the difference between what they depicted as fractious democracies and decisive Chinese governance, negative reports about the vaccine-rollout process in Europe, and disinformation alleging dangerous side effects of European and American vaccines. It also promoted traditional Chinese medicines for the treatment of COVID-19.[51] Again, the CCP was not the originator of these stories (nor was Russia in this case), but it used a growing social-media network to amplify messages that could undermine American and European credibility while offering a favourable view of China's handling of the pandemic.[52] Ultimately, however, there is no firm evidence that this effort was successful. Moreover, China suffered a setback when evidence emerged that its own vaccines, which were widely used globally, were far less effective than those that had been developed in the West.[53]

How successful were China's efforts to shape global perceptions about COVID-19? On the one hand, China was able during the pandemic to increase its presence in traditional forms of international media, such as television and print, as reflected in a 2021 survey of European journalists in which three-quarters of them said China had a visible presence in their national media, a significant increase in comparison with a similar survey conducted in 2019.[54] And most of this coverage was positive, with a majority of countries surveyed in 2020 saying China was being covered more favourably than before in their national media.[55] According to a study by the Nieman Lab at Harvard University, 'the overall increase in positivity [of stories] coincided with an uptick in Chinese outreach'.[56]

On the other hand, media presence is not the same as influence and did not translate into a more positive international opinion of China. China's attempts to improve its 'soft power' in Southeastern, Central and Eastern Europe, for example, where civil societies can be weak and oligarchies retain a strong influence, were largely focused on influential elites rather than the general public.[57] A YouGov opinion poll in 2020 found that a large majority of respondents in 25 different countries believed China had 'tried to hide the truth' about COVID-19 and could have prevented the spread of the virus if it had responded sooner. And a 2021 survey in 13 European countries found that opinions about China became much more negative as a result of the pandemic.[58]

During the pandemic, instead of creating new narratives or developing original messaging, China amplified and put its own spin on pre-existing narratives and stories. While these narratives enabled it to be aggressive in advancing claims that the US military was responsible for the pandemic, the CCP's goal was largely to deflect blame and protect itself. Many of the narratives amplified by China included disinformation about Taiwan's response to the pandemic or questioned the safety of Western vaccines.[59] China relied heavily on its diplomats to contribute to this amplification effect. For example, Graphika found that Chinese diplomats had amplified many of the fake accounts and fake stories in the networks it investigated, although it is unconfirmed that they knew these were fake.[60] These networks took advantage of Facebook's algorithm that created a 'filter bubble', showing users more of the same types of stories and information that confirmed their views.[61]

Conclusion

We were unable to examine how Chinese government narratives and social-media activity on platforms such as Weibo (China's main social-media platform) and WeChat resonated with the intended domestic audience, largely because of the difficulty of gauging public opinion in China. CCP domestic narratives, like those it propagates abroad, have tended to promote the reunification of China and Taiwan, to undermine Western democracies and to advance a favourable image of China as a world leader. Despite its digital information campaigns, the pandemic ultimately represented a source of embarrassment for China and jeopardised these efforts.

Again, though, we can envision scenarios in which social media could play a more escalatory role in future geopolitical crises. China's attempt during the pandemic to create chaos in the information space and confuse response options, for example, could have military implications in a future conflict, such as an invasion of Taiwan. China has also demonstrated that it will go to great lengths to protect its image. Yet there is no evidence that aggressive information campaigns during the pandemic have been anything other than counterproductive. When seeking to shape attitudes in Western countries, what can be achieved on social media will be limited by the role played by the main broadcasting and print media.

Unlike in the other crises described in this volume, the pandemic did not raise the prospect of military escalation but rather of information (and disinformation) escalation. It presented major challenges for China's international image, particularly with regard to its handling of the initial outbreak. Beijing's response was to craft a digital information campaign for international audiences portraying itself as having bought time for the rest of the world through its quick response, and then to deflect blame for the spread of the virus. Whereas Russia was already a well-established actor in spreading disinformation on social media, the pandemic saw a significant evolution in China's social-media activities and crisis behaviour. But as with Russian information efforts generally, the aggressiveness of its campaign turned out to be counterproductive. There is no clear evidence that Chinese disinformation and propaganda campaigns produced significantly positive results for the CCP. China's overall image abroad remains largely negative, and perceptions that China is to blame for the pandemic persist. Its sensitivity on the matter was illustrated when Australia demanded that the WHO instigate a full inquiry into how the pandemic began in China, leading to Beijing instigating a trade war.

Moreover, China's formal narrative as the COVID-19 crisis continued into 2021 and 2022 failed to have a positive impact not only with its international audience but also with its far more important domestic audience. China enacted a 'zero COVID' policy whereby anyone in proximity to someone who had tested positive was put into forced lockdown, which often had the result of isolating entire apartment buildings or locking down major metropolitan areas, such as Shanghai. These extreme measures became increasingly unpopular, with videos of riots and demonstrations circulating on Weibo. For example, in June 2022, when the Chinese Center for Disease Control and Prevention released a report stating that the Omicron variant was less dangerous than other forms of COVID-19, the public took to Weibo to oppose the strong measures, particularly in Shanghai. The report's hashtag was viewed 98m times in three days.[62] There were also many complaints on social media about the shortages of many types of food and other products – and also the lack of information – during the pandemic. The government's response was: 'Act faster, prevent spread and spillover, especially to Beijing.'[63] Having tried to turn COVID-19 into a story about the high quality of the CCP's leadership, by the end of 2022 the authorities were in full defensive mode, trying – and failing – to prevent the Chinese public (as well as the rest of the world) from seeing the level of domestic opposition their policies were generating. Having a high degree of control over social media did not enable the Chinese government to control an angry population.

In the end, whatever the messages being promoted on social media and elsewhere, the Chinese narrative clashed with reality – including the failure to suppress the virus while most other countries were moving on from the pandemic. So insistent had the authorities been about their success against COVID-19 that they could not let it appear that the virus was gaining the upper hand. Yet no matter how insistent the warnings about the dire consequences of the virus if it was left uncontrolled, the incessant testing and regular lockdowns eventually precipitated popular discontent. While the government responded to the demonstrations with customary repression, their scale was hard to ignore, especially as they began to incorporate a wider complaint about the country's lack of freedom. Moreover, importantly, it was difficult for the public to see when the lockdowns – with their adverse economic consequences – would ever stop. In December 2022, in an abrupt about-turn, the government abandoned the rules that it claimed had kept the virus in check. Inevitably the relief felt by the population was tinged with concern that in winter, and with much of the most vulnerable population not yet fully vaccinated, the virus would spread very quickly. A government unused to acknowledging trade-offs was now caught between accepting large numbers of deaths or continuing with its past practice of claiming that all was for the best, and that neither cases nor deaths were going up significantly – in which case what had been the point of the lockdowns?[64] This was an important demonstration of the limits of information campaigns. They cannot compensate for misconceived and poorly executed policy, and while they can attempt to frame an awkward reality in a much more positive way, they cannot alter it.

CHAPTER FIVE

Russia and the Ukraine crisis, 2013–23

The origins of the Ukraine crisis date to the break-up of the Soviet Union in December 1991. Once Ukraine became independent, it was pulled in opposite directions: much of the population, particularly in the west of the country, was drawn towards the European Union, whereas many in the east continued to feel some connection to Russia. Ukraine's leaders initially avoided choosing between Europe and Russia, but this became increasingly difficult as Russian President Vladimir Putin increased efforts to reassert Russian influence over Ukraine's foreign policy. Russian pressure increased in 2013 and led to a series of events – the Maidan protests in Kyiv, the annexation of Crimea and the sponsored secessionist movements in the Donbas in 2014 – culminating in the full military invasion in February 2022 and Ukraine's unexpectedly tough resistance.

The case of Ukraine is especially significant in understanding the role of social media and other digital tools during crises, given Russia's commitment to information campaigns as a vital instrument of modern conflict. Digital information campaigns have played an important role in Putin's strategy as a way of shoring up domestic support and pressuring the

Ukrainian leadership to capitulate by undermining its credibility and weakening its support in the West. In 2022, however, the Russian media campaign was no more successful than its military campaign. Support for Ukraine rose dramatically and remained high, at least in the West, while few Russian messages gained much traction. Only in the so-called 'Global South' did Russia have more success in this respect, although this was less because of the quality of its messaging than because of governments protecting their interests with Russia and disliking being lectured by Western governments, often judged to be hypocritical after their interventions in Afghanistan and Iraq. Ukrainian President Volodymyr Zelenskyy accepted some responsibility for failing to get Ukraine's message across to India and much of Africa, and noted a successful Russian disinformation campaign in Latin America, which Ukraine was trying to combat.[1]

The Ukraine crisis provides important insights into the role of digital information operations in contemporary conflict, illustrating how an authoritarian regime uses such operations both to reinforce its narratives aimed at the domestic audience and to try to undermine an adversary. Online information campaigns have been evident at a number of key moments: in November 2013, when Facebook was a major organising tool for protesters gathering in the Maidan in Kyiv; in the spring of 2014, as Russian-backed militias seized parts of eastern Ukraine; in July 2014, when a Malaysia Airlines passenger aircraft was shot down by one of those militias using a Russian *Buk* surface-to-air missile; in the build-up to the 2022 invasion; and then during the ensuing war. In 2013, as the crisis escalated, Russia used a variety of digital information tools – bot networks, troll farms and pro-Russia news outlets. Since then, social-media and disinformation tactics have evolved significantly, and Russia has moved away from troll farms but continues to rely heavily on digital information campaigns and both offensive and defensive narratives as part of a wider strategy to return Ukraine to its sphere of influence.[2]

Russia's authoritarianism is intertwined with its disinformation and social-media strategy. Despite initial hopes that social media might facilitate pro-democracy movements, such as the Arab Spring, authoritarian governments have learned to control the internet more effectively over the past decade, especially when it comes to monitoring and shutting down opposition voices and deflecting domestic discontent. They have also used social media to apply pressure on democracies. Russia has sought to do this by using fake news to confuse public debate in the West and undermine trust in the media there.[3] To challenge American supremacy, Moscow has advanced the narrative that it is an anti-Western power, while also being opportunistic in capitalising on pre-existing narratives and networks hostile to liberal society or ideals.[4] Through the years of the Ukraine conflict since 2013, Moscow has taken advantage of groups, both within Russia and elsewhere, to construct an information ecosystem that can expose a wider audience to pro-Russian views in support of its ambitions. Even before 2022, however, the limits of this ecosystem had become apparent. And during 2022, Moscow's information campaign failed to generate support for Russian military objectives, particularly in its efforts to persuade Western countries to end their active support for Ukraine.

The lead-up to the crisis: Ukraine's relationship with Europe, and Russian disinformation

Leonid Kuchma, president of independent Ukraine from 1994 to 2005, advocated close ties with Russia. His government was plagued by allegations of corruption and other scandals. In one of the more prominent incidents, reported by Human Rights

Watch and dubbed 'Kuchmagate', the president's former security guard taped a series of conversations in which Kuchma authorised the sale of military equipment to Iraq in violation of a UN arms embargo.[5] He was also implicated in the killing of a journalist, Georgy Gongadze, who was investigating corruption claims against him, though the charges were dismissed by a Ukrainian court in December 2014.[6] In the lead-up to the presidential election in the autumn of 2004, Kuchma supported the candidacy of his prime minister, Viktor Yanukovych. Both Kuchma and Yanukovych had been moving Ukraine towards formally joining the Commonwealth of Independent States and closer integration with Russia.

Events surrounding the election proved to be particularly dramatic. In September 2004, opposition leader Viktor Yushchenko fell ill and was found to have been poisoned with dioxin, leaving him disfigured and scarred.[7] In a run-off between Yanukovych and Yushchenko in November, Yanukovych was declared the winner. On 21 November, Yushchenko called for protests against the election results due to suspicions – and evidence – of fraud, and his supporters descended on the Maidan square, parliament and other government buildings in central Kyiv. Observers from the Organization for Security and Co-operation in Europe (OSCE) reported extensive election fraud, including voter intimidation and the stuffing of ballot boxes.[8] As the protests spread across the country, many local governments refused to accept the election results, and on 3 December the Supreme Court called for a new election.[9] When the new run-off took place in January 2005, Yushchenko was declared the winner. Seven years later, after Yanukovych had become president in 2010, Ukrainians protested the outcome of the 2012 parliamentary elections because of claims of Russian-backed fraud.[10]

In 2008, Ukraine agreed in principle to an association agreement with the EU. However, the EU became lukewarm following Yanukovych's victory over Yulia Timoshenko in the 2010 presidential election, with member states expressing concerns when Timoshenko was subsequently imprisoned on the grounds that as prime minister (2007–10) she had abused her office to broker a gas deal with Russia in 2009. Additionally, Ukraine initially rejected any preconditions for the agreement, including the release of Timoshenko, but Yanukovych eventually agreed that Ukraine would work to meet the EU's requirements. At the same time, however, Yanukovych was in negotiations with Russia to join its own customs union, the Eurasian Economic Union (EEU).

Putin insisted that Ukraine had to choose between the EU and the EEU. In 2013 he exploited Ukraine's economic and energy vulnerability in an attempt to coerce the generally pro-Russian Yanukovych into abandoning the EU path. In November 2013 – after months of stalling, and in the face of intense economic pressure from Russia – Yanukovych announced that Ukraine would not push ahead with the association agreement with the EU.[11] The announcement led to protests throughout Ukraine, with the biggest ones taking place in the Maidan in Kyiv. By December the number of protesters there had risen to about 800,000. Yanukovych failed in his efforts to suppress them by force and eventually, on 22 February 2014, fled the country. The protests – now known as the 'Revolution of Dignity' – prompted a harsh Russian response, including the annexation of Crimea in mid-March and also the fomenting of unrest in eastern Ukraine, backed with violence and leading to two pro-Russian so-called 'people's republics' being proclaimed in the Ukrainian *oblasts* of Donetsk and Luhansk in the eastern region of the Donbas. Russia's attacks on Ukrainian sovereignty led to Western economic sanctions.

After years of conflict in eastern Ukraine and various unsuccessful efforts involving international mediation, in 2021 Putin made clear his desire to reshape the future of Ukraine and its constitutional arrangements. This went beyond the status of the areas in the Donbas under separatist control: he wanted to reorient Ukraine towards Russia, away from the EU and NATO. Having failed to achieve his declared objectives, which included various restrictions on NATO's posture in Eastern Europe, on 24 February 2022 Putin launched a full-scale invasion of Ukraine. The initial aim was to depose President Zelenskyy's government and replace it with one more favourable to the Kremlin, making Ukraine a de facto Russian colony. When Ukraine's armed forces succeeded in repelling the invaders from around Kyiv, Putin decided to concentrate on acquiring territory for Russia in eastern and southern Ukraine.

As Ukraine's forces grew stronger, with substantial Western support, Russia's forces suffered a series of reverses in the land war and were unable to consolidate their positions. From the early stages of the war Russia mounted attacks against Ukraine's infrastructure. These became more focused and effective from September 2022 onwards, denying many Ukrainians access to electricity and water for extended periods. Russia also sought to push against Western support for the war, causing havoc in international energy markets. In the information domain, Russia's campaigns were intended to drive home the message in the West and elsewhere that Ukraine was an undeserving cause and that relief from economic pain would only come if support for Ukraine were abandoned. These information campaigns also sought to encourage the view that continuing to support Ukraine in the war carried high risks, including the possibility of nuclear escalation.

After Ukraine made some progress in liberating territory through a counter-offensive in September 2022, Russia escalated by moving to annex the *oblasts* of Kherson, Zaporizhzhia, Donetsk and Luhansk, as it had done with Crimea in 2014, even though it did not fully occupy those areas; backing this with a partial mobilisation of military reservists; and also becoming more systematic in its attacks on critical infrastructure. Aware that Ukraine was planning its own spring offensive, which would be backed by an influx of Western weaponry, Russia embarked in January 2023 on an offensive of its own. This ended in May with Russia having made minimal gains and with Ukraine starting to take the military initiative. Russian pressure on Europe through an energy crunch and its attempts to coerce Kyiv through attacks on infrastructure had also failed. The question now was whether Ukraine would be able to take the initiative sufficiently to liberate even more of its territory while sustaining Western support. The first weeks of the Ukrainian offensive saw pro-Russian websites seeking to demonstrate that it was failing catastrophically, while the Ukrainian government tried to convey the message that it was bound to take time and that Russian capabilities had to be degraded before it would be possible to break through Russian lines.[12]

At the time of writing, despite continuing uncertainties about Ukraine's prospects in the ground war, its determination to fight for its sovereignty and independence remained unwavering, as did Western economic and military support for its efforts. Russia's ability to shape events was undermined by military incompetence and acts of barbarity against civilians in occupied territory, confusion over its war aims, and the general crudity of its strategy. Although Russia had come to be seen by many Western analysts as a master of social-media operations, Ukraine was winning the information war – at least in the countries where it mattered most. Zelenskyy, unlike Putin, was a natural performer who knew how to tailor messages to particular audiences. There was also a clear purpose behind all his information activities, which was to make the case for even greater levels of outside support. He successfully depicted Ukraine as a brave victim fighting back against unprovoked aggression. Antipathy towards Russia and its evident aggression, strengthened by the Western media's direct reporting of Russian war crimes, meant that it was less a case of Zelenskyy having to undermine pro-Russian sentiment in Western countries than building upon pro-Ukraine sentiment. He simply had a better story to tell.

Before Moscow unleashed all-out war against Ukraine, Peter Singer and Emerson Brooking described Russia's approach to social media as akin to a 'Schrödinger's war', intended to warp perceptions, sow confusion and make the audience question reality. In 2014, during the early part of the crisis, Russia's goal was to create 'a violent, confusing, paralyzing mess'.[13] In this respect there seemed to be a natural role for social media when it came to manipulating information and forging narratives in an attempt to shape perceptions. In testimony to the US Congressional Commission on Security and Cooperation in Europe in 2017, one witness referred to the 'smoke and mirrors' of Russia's information operations, considering them to be 'a primary means of power projection'.[14] Other descriptions of the Russian government's social-media activity at this time included 'guerrilla approach', 'scattershot' and 'piecemeal'.[15]

In 2020, former senior US official Brad Roberts prophetically described Russia's theory of victory in Ukraine as:

> making Western publics and decisionmakers fearful of the high costs of taking [Ukraine] back and … shaping their information environments with tailored messages. Russian experts appear to believe that, in such a contingency, NATO would be divided about how to respond, its publics would be fearful of war, and these factors can be exploited with actions

illustrating the potential costs and risks and thereby reduce the probability of a concerted NATO response.[16]

Two years later, after the invasion, information and psychological operations would indeed prove to be core components of Russia's strategy.

The events of 2013–14: the Maidan, Crimea and MH17

Social media was a prominent tool during the 2013–14 protests, being used as an organising platform by the protesters but also by pro-Yanukovych and pro-Russia groups. The protests were initiated via Facebook. In response to Yanukovych's announcement that Ukraine would no longer pursue the association agreement with the EU, Ukrainian journalist Mustafa Nayyem posted this message on Facebook:

> Well, let's get serious. Who today is ready to come to Maidan before midnight? 'Likes' don't count. Only comments under this post with the words, 'I am ready.' As soon as we get more than a thousand, we will organize ourselves.[17]

The hashtag #Euromaidan became a call to action and a shared moniker for those organising the hundreds of thousands of protesters who gathered in Kyiv and other cities throughout Ukraine.[18]

Facebook remained an important means of communication throughout, particularly in the winter and spring of 2013–14 when the Berkut riot police began their crackdown against the Maidan protesters, and in helping forge a narrative about the Ukrainian people's bravery in standing up to corruption and foreign intervention in elections. The protesters relied heavily on Facebook groups such as Euromaidan SOS, which became an organising hub and information service run by some 250 volunteers. In this stage of the initial crisis, social media helped shape the conflict by facilitating protests and adding to the pressure on Yanukovych. It should be noted, however, that the majority of the Ukrainian population at the time did not use social media at all, and also that social media was liable to give the protesters a certain degree of false confidence. Ironically, however, this may have contributed to their ultimate success. As one study put it:

> The sense of unanimity and popular support the opposition believed they enjoyed turned out to be, to a certain degree, an illusion created not only by a subset of the population with access to the Internet, but in some cases by well-orchestrated spam bot campaigns.[19]

On 21 January 2014, in an incident believed to have been orchestrated by pro-Russian groups within Ukraine, many Maidan protesters close to the scene of a violent clash with police received the same text message: 'Dear subscriber, you are registered as a participant in a mass disturbance.' Though this did not deter the protesters, it indicated that they were under surveillance through phone and data networks.[20]

Meanwhile, Russian military spies were creating fake personas and accounts on Facebook and VKontakte, a Russian social-media platform, pretending to be ordinary Ukrainians voicing opposition to the protests. In one example, on 22 February, 'Ivan Galitsin' posted this comment in response to an article in a British newspaper:

> There was a coup in Ukraine … I live in Kiev. I was on the Maidan, but peaceful protests ended two months

ago, when we were displaced by armed nationalists. It's a nightmare. Fascists came to us again 70 years after the Second World War. I do not want this future for Ukraine.[21]

Claims of fascism became, and remain, an integral part of Russia's narrative about events in Ukraine. During the 2013–14 protests, blogs became one of the most important social-media platforms – one of them, LiveJournal, made up 23% of Russian-language social-media posts.[22]

After Yanukovych fled to exile in Russia in February 2014, an interim government was formed until Petro Poroshenko took over following presidential elections in May. On 1 March, Yanukovych sent a letter to Putin asking for the Russian armed forces to 'restore the rule of law, peace, order, stability and protection of the population of Ukraine'.[23] The letter was presented to the UN by Russia's permanent representative Vitaly Churkin on 4 March, with Moscow claiming Russian nationals and Russian-language speakers were at risk in Ukraine because of the unconstitutional change of government. This supposed threat became the basis for the nationalist appeal to the Russian domestic audience, aimed at justifying the intervention in Ukrainian affairs that culminated in the 2022 invasion. In 2014, 15–20% of Ukrainians identified as ethnic Russians, mostly in the east and the south of the country.[24] A related theme was that the protests in Ukraine were part of a Western-backed 'coup' designed to undermine Russia's regional influence, including by putting at risk the Black Sea Fleet based at the port of Sevastopol.[25]

These themes were prominent in late February, when pro-Russian militias backed by Russian special forces took over the Crimean parliament. They pushed through a referendum on 16 March that approved Crimea joining the Russian Federation. A month later, armed men seized government offices in Donetsk and Luhansk, declaring two 'people's republics' there. Putin initially denied Russian involvement in these events, but on 17 April he acknowledged that Russian troops had been present in Crimea before the referendum to support pro-Russian 'self-defence forces' there, and it was evident that the leaders of the rebellion were largely Russian.

The crisis escalated in eastern Ukraine in spring 2014 as militias seized towns throughout the Donbas region. They held elections within the so-called people's republics in Donetsk and Luhansk. Gradually it dawned on the militia leaders that Putin had no intention of annexing these territories but instead wanted them to be autonomous entities within Ukraine, so he could use them to put pressure on the new government in Kyiv.[26] Ukraine's armed forces were becoming more effective as they tried to recover lost territory, beginning a major offensive in the east in early July and retaking a number of towns. At this point Putin decided that regular forces were needed to prevent the total defeat of the militias. A report by Bellingcat found that on 16 July, for the first time, Russian artillery fired at Ukrainian forces from inside Russia. There was no pretence anymore that this was a civil war.

Interestingly, social media did not play a prominent role during the annexation of Crimea or the escalation in eastern Ukraine. Although Russia invested significantly in trolls in the lead-up to and following the Crimea referendum, paying them to advance a pro-Russia narrative on social media including Twitter, VKontakte and blogs, those stories were predominantly spread through traditional media, particularly television.[27] According to a study by the analyst Lennart Maschmeyer:

> There is no evidence of co-ordinated large-scale digital disinformationcampaigns,northatdigitaldisinformation

contributed to the success of the Crimean operation. In fact, a recent study found that the vast majority of Twitter content relating to the Crimean crisis challenged disinformation narratives. Social media disinformation involved ad-hoc efforts to confuse Crimean audiences and leaders rather than long-term campaigns to sway public opinion … while there is a pervasive lack of evidence that digital media facilitated the dissemination of disinformation that contributed to the Crimean take-over, there is a strong indication that traditional media provided more effective channels and at greater scale.[28]

The state has a complete monopoly on non-digital media sources in Russia, and television led the way in spreading disinformation about events in 2014. One prominent story came from Channel One, which interviewed a young woman fleeing from eastern Ukraine who claimed she had seen Ukrainian soldiers crucify a three-year-old boy in a public square; she said the boy's mother had been forced to watch, before being tied to a Ukrainian tank and dragged behind it until she died. The story reached millions of viewers and was one of the most commonly cited by pro-Russian groups. But it was untrue. An online group dedicated to combatting disin-formation in Ukraine, StopFake, later debunked the story by spotting numerous inconsistencies.[29]

Moscow adopted a range of tactics. In its information campaign it predominantly used Twitter, Facebook, VKontakte and blogs to promote disinformation and alternative narra-tives about the Ukraine crisis. Most of the activity was by government-sponsored actors, such as the Russian foreign-intelligence agency, paid trolls, and bots. The disinformation campaigns on social media were largely decentralised, with troll farms, bot networks, fake accounts and pro-Russia news organisations mostly operating independently from each other. Mark Galeotti referred to this as 'authoritarian entrepreneurialism', whereby a variety of actors serve the Kremlin as they see fit.[30]

An important feature of the crisis was the creation of a disinformation ecosystem whereby Russia linked various news organisations and used social media to amplify fake stories. This included established platforms such as Channel One and RT News along with organisations that were probably backed by the Kremlin, including News Front and South Front.[31] This system made it particularly difficult for social-media organisations and foreign governments to prevent the spread of disinformation. Twitter and Facebook blocked English-language posts from News Front, among other sources, and the Ukrainian government blocked the majority of sources of Russian disinformation. The EU responded by promoting 'media literacy' and correcting Russian fake news, with some success, before banning Russian TV stations more broadly following the 2022 invasion. As of 2022, other efforts to combat Russian disinformation were being led by open-source intelligence and investigative organisations such as Bellingcat and StopFake.

In the early stages of the crisis the Ukrainian government tried various measures to shut down Russia's information warfare. These included investigations into bot and troll farms, blocking Russian news sources and shutting off access to certain social networks. Ukraine banned Russian television for the first time in 2014, and in 2017 blocked a number of Russian-affiliated social-media networks and websites as part of a sanctions regime against Moscow. Later, in February 2021, it blocked three major Russian news channels on the grounds of preventing the spread of disinformation. Massive bot farms were identified: one in southern Ukraine with 4,000 servers belonging to private companies in 63 countries, discovered in

April 2016 with German assistance; one known as 'Sapphire', sponsored by Russian foreign intelligence, which spread disinformation and called for anti-government protests in Ukraine, discovered in March 2019; and one operated by Russian citizens and displaced persons from Donbas, managing more than 500 accounts, which was identified in January 2020.

A 2018 RAND Corporation study on Russian disinformation and social media described Moscow as aiming 'to leverage shared elements of the post-Soviet experience in order to drive wedges between ethnic Russian or Russian-speaking populations who reside in [other] states and their host governments'.[32] These audiences, particularly in eastern Ukraine, were encouraged to believe that it was the West that was launching information warfare in an attempt to destabilise Russia.[33] Russia was not introducing a new narrative to these audiences, but rather providing new material to reinforce pre-existing ones.

There was one important and salutary lesson indicating the limits of Russian information campaigns. On 17 July 2014, Malaysia Airlines flight MH17, carrying 283 passengers (the majority from the Netherlands) and 15 crew, was shot down over eastern Ukraine by a *Buk* surface-to-air missile fired by a Russian crew working with a pro-Russian Ukrainian militia. Militia leaders initially boasted on social media that they had shot down a Ukrainian Air Force plane, only to delete their posts as it became apparent what had happened. Most observers could immediately see where responsibility probably lay, despite the militia leaders coming up with the story that MH17 had been attacked by a Ukrainian plane that they then shot down with their missile. Later, Russia and the separatists advanced a variety of other theories – one was that MH17 was on the wrong path; another claimed the shooting-down was a false-flag operation, an idea that spread widely across social media.[34] Investigations in the aftermath of the incident – the most important of which was conducted by Dutch prosecutors, who had access to intercepts of phone calls between militia leaders – were able to piece together the sequence of events. Independent groups, including Bellingcat, were subsequently able to prove the missile had originated in Russia, and Bellingcat later produced additional evidence showing the *Buk* had been operated on 17 July by a Russian anti-aircraft-missile brigade.[35]

By 2022, Russian attempts to deflect responsibility for the MH17 incident had failed. The Kremlin's messages were inconsistent, and dependent on denial and distraction.[36] Russia used the incident as an opportunity to blame the West for interfering in Ukraine and to criticise the Western media for its portrayal of the events.[37] In the words of journalist Peter Pomerantsev, Russia was 'trying not so much to convince viewers of any one version of events, but rather to leave them confused, paranoid, and passive – living in a Kremlin-controlled virtual reality that can no longer be mediated or debated by any appeal to "truth"'.[38] It was denial by obfuscation. Within Russia, the various alternative explanations for the fate of MH17 were effective: polling suggests Russians still believe it was someone else's responsibility.[39] Yet despite all the effort put into insisting that the obvious explanation was false, the truth is now largely accepted outside Russia. In October 2022, four of the perpetrators were tried (*in absentia*) in The Hague and three were found guilty.[40]

One of those convicted was Igor Girkin (aka Strelkov), who had been one of the most prominent militia leaders in Ukraine in the spring and summer of 2014. Having played a role in the annexation of Crimea, his objective was to encourage a similar integration of eastern Ukraine with Russia, whereas Moscow wanted to keep these areas as an irritant in Ukrainian politics.

Girkin's wayward statements and behaviour, including his role in the MH17 incident, led Moscow to fear he could prompt a backlash in Russia against what nationalists perceived as the government's lack of ambition. Moscow ordered him to return to Russia. Later, following the 2022 invasion, when Russia's war aims accorded more with his own, Girkin became an active blogger, making downbeat assessments of Russia's military situation and criticising the authorities for incompetence and a half-hearted approach to winning the war.[41]

As an instrument of foreign policy during the crisis, Russia's digital information campaigns largely failed to divide Ukraine or NATO support. Where there was already pro-Russian or anti-Western sentiment, this could be reinforced, but elsewhere Russia was not trusted and its propaganda was not readily believed. The MH17 incident provides an interesting contrast to the shooting down of the Ukrainian aircraft in Iran in January 2020. In the latter case, after initial reluctance to acknowledge responsibility, the authorities in Tehran realised that this could no longer be avoided. The tragedy therefore contributed to the de-escalation of the crisis. In the case of MH17 the Russians drew the conclusion that they needed to get a better grip on the actions of the militias in eastern Ukraine, but they did not let up on their offensive until they had consolidated the territory they controlled. Then they moved to de-escalate, using normal diplomatic channels. A ceasefire agreement was reached in Minsk in September, which was refined, after further fighting, in a second agreement, Minsk II, in February 2015. Minsk II anticipated that Russian forces would withdraw from the areas in which they were present, which would be integrated back into Ukraine. Its terms were not implemented, however, and fighting continued in and around the ceasefire lines. From 2015–22, Moscow actively sowed narratives both in the Donbas and in the West about Russia and its interests in Ukraine. In addition to an unsettled dispute, the other main legacy of the aggressive and often cynical nature of Moscow's information campaign was increased distance between Russia and the West.

All-out war, 2022–23: lead-up and invasion

During the second half of 2021 and into early 2022 there was a major build-up of Russian forces around the borders of Ukraine, including in Belarus. As the Ukrainian government and Western analysts tried to discern Russian intentions, the Kremlin relied on formal narratives, mostly defensive in nature, denying an intention to invade but claiming that southern and eastern Ukraine were really part of Russia and that the government in Kyiv was illegitimate and seeking to join NATO to gain support for taking back Crimea. In July 2021 Putin had published an essay insisting that Russians and Ukrainians were one people and that the break-up of the Soviet Union had produced artificial borders.[42] In a speech just three days before the invasion, Putin claimed Ukraine remained an 'inalienable' part of Russian culture and history.[43] In the same speech he alleged Ukraine was pursuing an independent nuclear-weapons programme, and the following day added that if Ukraine developed nuclear weapons, it would be a 'strategic threat' to Russia. After the invasion he frequently returned to all these themes, such as on 10 June 2022, when he likened himself to Peter the Great and compared Russia's attack on Ukraine to its reclaiming of lands from Sweden in the Great Northern War.

On 17 December 2021, Russia suggested various measures to defuse the developing tension, including formal security guarantees from NATO, a treaty that would impose a blanket ban on the deployment of short- and intermediate-range missiles, a ban on any NATO deployments in post-1997 NATO states, and no further NATO expansion.[44] Little of this offered much scope for negotiations; instead the aim seemed to be to isolate Ukraine. On

10 January 2022, US deputy secretary of state Wendy Sherman and Russian Deputy Foreign Minister Sergei Ryabkov met for seven hours to discuss Russia's proposals and indicated afterwards that there was mutual interest in returning to something similar to the Intermediate-Range Nuclear Forces Treaty. That same week, Russian and NATO officials met in Brussels, and with the OSCE in Vienna, in the hope of de-escalating the crisis. While Russia would no doubt have been delighted if NATO had acceded to all its demands, there was never much prospect of that happening. Russia waited until 24 February before launching its invasion, possibly to avoid acting before the end of the Beijing Winter Olympics in deference to Xi Jinping.

Putin's justification focused on the artificiality of Ukraine, the illegitimacy of its government and the threat to Russian-language speakers in the Donbas.[45] According to this narrative, the Ukrainian governments of Poroshenko (2014–19) and later Zelenskyy (2019–) were fascists and 'Banderovtsy', a term associated with paramilitary groups that supported the Germans in Ukraine during the Second World War.[46] These accusations were particularly prominent in social-media accounts later found to be associated with the Russian armed forces.[47]

A consistent theme before and during the invasion was that Ukrainian troops were committing atrocities, which carried echoes of the crucifixion story from 2014. Russia flooded the digital information space with a series of fake news stories, including photographs and video footage subsequently proven to have been altered. Though intended to undermine the Ukrainian government, the narrative was aimed mainly at the Russian domestic audience and at the pro-Russian public in eastern Ukraine and elsewhere in Eastern Europe, especially those on the extreme political right or political left who might be identified as anti-Western.[48] One story in 2014 claimed a four-year-old boy in Donetsk had been killed by a Ukrainian drone strike, but multiple eyewitnesses later confirmed the death had been an accident and did not involve a drone.[49] In early December 2021, using videos later proven to be fake, several Facebook pages claimed Ukrainian border forces were shooting at refugees.[50] These stories became more frequent in the days preceding the invasion, with increasing references on Russian state TV to 'genocide' against ethnic Russians in Donetsk and Luhansk, matching similar patterns in the lead-ups to the military interventions in Crimea in 2014 and Georgia in 2008.[51] And on 20 February the leadership of the Donetsk People's Republic (DNR) published photos of a car explosion, claiming it was an assassination attempt against the head of DNR policy, but fact-checkers later demonstrated that the explosion was staged and that the car's number plates were fake.[52]

Another theme in the lead-up to the invasion and afterwards was that of chemical and biological weapons. On 21 December 2021 the Russian defence minister, Sergei Shoigu, alleged that US mercenaries had brought chemical weapons into Ukraine.[53] Russia also pushed a narrative about the US operating biological-weapons facilities across Ukraine.[54] This was one of the few claims that gained international traction – particularly with China, as it overlapped with the CCP's desire to present the US as the source of COVID-19.

The Russians used the letter 'Z' to symbolise the invasion, with the letter first appearing on Russian military vehicles gathering near the Ukrainian border. One explanation was that Russian troops had painted the letter (along with various other symbols and shapes) on their vehicles to distinguish them from similar Ukrainian vehicles.[55] On 2 March, Russia's Ministry of Defence posted a picture with a 'Z' on Twitter with the caption 'For victory', then followed up three days later with further 'Z' pictures accompanied by the captions 'We finish wars' and 'For the children of Donbas'.[56] While the 'Z' symbol seemed, at least initially, to gain some traction within Russia itself, it appeared very largely to fail as an effective symbol galvanising support for the Russian invasion elsewhere.

Ukraine was active in challenging Russia's digital information campaigns. On 23 February, the day before the invasion, Zelenskyy appealed directly to the Russian people in a 20-minute speech, asking them to question the Kremlin's motives. Once the invasion began, Ukraine's Ministry of Internal Affairs established a hotline for Russian citizens to get information about individual Russian soldiers captured or missing.[57] In March, Zelenskyy called on Russian soldiers to surrender, promising they would be treated humanely, and expressed gratitude for the actions of those in Russia who were still trying to express the truth and fight disinformation.[58] On 1 April he called on Russian parents to resist conscription in order to save their sons' lives.[59] Later, during the Ukrainian counter-offensive in September, he called on Russian citizens to resist Putin's mobilisation and its soldiers to desert, and reiterated the assurance that soldiers who surrendered would be treated well.[60]

In addition to sustaining Ukrainian morale, Zelenskyy's main effort was to ensure that he maximised international support for Ukraine's resistance to Russian aggression. This was the theme behind all his messaging. He took every opportunity to speak to foreign audiences, including governments, parliaments and potentially influential groups within civil society. He proved to be an effective and charismatic media performer – unlike Putin, whose public statements were dull and formulaic, especially as it became barely credible to promise an eventual victory. When Zelenskyy delivered speeches to national parliaments he tailored his remarks to connect effectively with each audience. His message was consistent throughout, starting from his reported comment on the first day of the invasion when he was offered help in escaping from Kyiv: 'The fight is here; I need ammunition, not a ride.' He constantly made the point that Ukraine was fighting for civilised values and to uphold international law, and urgently required military and economic assistance. On this basis, given the amount of military assistance Ukraine has received, its media campaign could be judged a success.

Immediately after the invasion, Zelenskyy and his team took to social media and shared videos of him walking calmly around Kyiv. The Ukrainian leadership used social media not only to show the world what was happening in the wake of Russian aggression but also to pressure social-media and technology companies to aid their cause. In early March the then-minister for digital transformation, Mykhailo Fedorov, requested that Apple block app-store access in Russia, directing a tweet at CEO Tim Cook that said: 'They kill our children, now kill their access!'[61] That same month, Fedorov tweeted at Elon Musk: 'While your rockets successfully land from space – Russian rockets attack Ukrainian civil people! We ask you to provide Ukraine with Starlink stations and to address sane Russians to stand.'[62] Within hours, according to Musk, Starlink was up and running in Ukraine.

As well as seeking ways to rally NATO and other Western support, Ukraine's information campaigns also featured disinformation. For example, its September 2022 counter-offensive benefitted from what one Ukrainian official described as 'a big special disinformation operation' that led many to believe Ukraine would focus solely on attacking Russian forces in the south, when they were also developing a counter-offensive focused on Kharkiv in the north.[63]

Ukraine's publicising of egregious and criminal Russian behaviour was of particular importance in gaining support and explaining why the country both needed arms and was reluctant to concede any of its territory to provide Putin with a diplomatic 'off-ramp'. This gained in effect after Russian forces were pushed back from around Kyiv, leaving behind evidence of atrocities against those caught in a temporary occupation. The US government, meanwhile, consistently challenged Putin's narrative about 'de-Nazification', and the State Department supported a statement from 140 international historians condemning Russia's 'equation of the Ukrainian state with the Nazi regime to justify its unprovoked aggression'.[64] As part of this counter-disinformation campaign, Western officials also shared information about Russia's military activities and warned about 'false flag' operations, potentially involving the use of chemical weapons.[65] The European Expert Association also proved to be a particularly useful resource, identifying a series of unsubstantiated Russian claims, including 'Ukraine is planning to attack some separatist-held territories using chemical weapons', 'the Ukrainian Army is preparing to attack Donbas' and 'nuclear power plants are at the centre of a US plot'.[66]

Ukraine's use of social media revealed two potential challenges not only for Kyiv but also for future digital information campaigns. Firstly, there was concern about a limited attention span, with the target audience possibly requiring increasingly innovative forms of messaging – a form of digital escalation – to remain receptive to the narrative. A *Foreign Policy* analysis in August 2022 observed, for example, that 'maintaining a compelling narrative remains important as the information war on the ground makes it difficult to verify even basic facts … As the war grinds on in the east and Ukraine plans a counteroffensive in the south, Zelensky and his advisors have continued to find ways to keep the West's eyes on the conflict.'[67] This would prove not to be a serious issue, however. The war remained an important and consequential story.

Secondly, and more seriously, there were the implications of dependence on private actors and organisations for communications and information campaigns, with Elon Musk in particular playing a prominent role. In September 2022, for example, Musk announced that Starlink would no longer be able to reliably provide internet access in Ukraine and asked the US government to pay the costs of keeping it going. Musk estimated that the 20,000 Starlink terminals donated to Ukraine would cost the company US$100m.[68] The uproar that followed persuaded Musk to continue the service, however. Later, in 2023, Musk would prevent his Starlink terminals from supporting Ukrainian operations that he saw as risking escalation. Furthermore, following Musk's acquisition of Twitter in October 2022, the platform became easier for pro-Russian propagandists to access.

Few governments were prepared to disseminate Russia's propaganda messages. Though Moscow, Tehran and Beijing have occasionally colluded in spreading disinformation – for example with regard to COVID-19, as demonstrated in Chapter Four – there was not much evidence of this in the case of Ukraine. Beijing did, however, help advance the Russian narrative that the US had established biological-weapons facilities in Ukraine, which fitted both the Russian narrative that Washington had fostered an imminent security danger to Russia within Ukraine and the Chinese narrative that it was in fact US biological research, not Chinese, that posed a threat to global wellbeing. On 8 March 2022, for example, the then-spokesperson for the Chinese foreign ministry, Zhao Lijian, made a statement that is worth quoting at length as it is evidence of the overlap of authoritarian disinformation campaigns across issues:

> I would also like to stress that the biological military activities of the US in Ukraine are merely the tip of the iceberg. Using such pretexts as cooperating to reduce biological safety risks and strengthening

global public health, the US has 336 biological labs in 30 countries under its control. 336, you heard me right. It also conducted many biological military activities at the Fort Detrick base at home…. What is the true intention of the US? What has it done specifically? The international community has long-held doubts. However, the US has kept stonewalling, and even dismissing the international community's doubts as spreading disinformation. Besides, the US has been standing alone in obstructing the establish-ment of a Biological Weapons Convention (BWC) verification mechanism and refusing verification of its biological facilities at home and abroad for the past two decades. This has led to deeper concern of the international community. Once again we urge the US to give a full account of its biological mili-tary activities at home and abroad and subject itself to multilateral verification.[69]

Other than this claim, which suits its own purposes in denying its culpability for the pandemic, China gave only luke-warm support for Russia's war aims (it abstained in UN votes). As the Russian military campaign faltered in the wake of the invasion, Beijing began to distance itself more.

Digital information campaigns and crisis management in Ukraine

The point cannot be overemphasised that putting considerable effort and resources into an information campaign does not necessarily lead to success. Narratives such as those pushed by Russia may cause confusion for a while, but if they do not stack up, especially in situations where close attention is being paid to events on the ground, they will fail.

The Russian government's information operations during crises, including its use of social media, are part of a larger strategy to undermine the credibility of Western governments and liberal norms.[70] Maria Snegovaya described this larger strategy as one of 'reflexive control', an old Soviet term, whereby Russia shapes adversaries' perceptions so that they take actions favourable to it, even if they are stronger. In theory this could mean Russia winning a war without firing a shot. In the case of the Ukrainian crisis, reflexive control has included denial and deception to create confusion about the presence or activities of Russian troops, pointing to Western hypocrisy about foreign intervention (given NATO's previous involvement in Kosovo, for example) and exaggerating claims about Russia's military prowess.[71] Through disinformation Russia has sought to create a 'perception hack' so as to give the *impression* it has interfered with an election or a political campaign or a military operation, and that alone is enough to sow doubt and influence an adversary's actions.[72] This approach has defensive elements, with plausible deniability, but it is also offensive in seeking to undermine Western narratives and expose the vulnerabilities of Western governments.[73]

Yet while social media can create confusion by offering multiple platforms for spreading disinformation, this confusion does not necessarily shape a crisis or influence its outcome. Before the 2022 invasion, Russian tactics were most successful when picking up and amplifying themes already present in debates in the target countries. Disinformation spread via social media largely reinforced pre-existing views and was targeted at the Russian domestic audience or the Russian-speaking diaspora in Eastern Europe. Even in the narrative wars surrounding Ukraine, traditional means of communication, particularly television, were the main influencers. As one study of the conflict put it, 'TV is king'.[74] Russia's tactics evolved after the beginning of the Ukraine crisis, and by 2022 it was no longer relying as heavily on content from troll farms.[75]

Russia's general approach to disinformation was 'opportunistic', with the goal of sowing distrust in democratic forms of government and undermining the credibility of the outcomes of democratic processes.[76] Beyond that, it struggled to develop and maintain a strong focus in its information campaigns. Its announced objectives have shifted during the course of the war. As it struggled to prevail in battle it not only blamed NATO for supplying weapons but sought to present Ukraine as a 'puppet' of the alliance, with no agency of its own. Yet it still spoke of Kyiv as having a 'neo-Nazi' agenda. The war was a 'special military operation', which suggested something limited, yet it also required the country to be put on a war footing.

Moscow therefore ended up running multiple campaigns at once. Few of these had the impact it desired. There was a degree of experimentation as Russia sought to learn from its successes and failures and identify which pieces of disinformation were the most contagious.[77] It did not go to great lengths to hide its disinformation efforts. Its bombardment of the information space continued apace, reflecting perhaps its lack of interest in trying to improve its own image or attract foreign audiences to the Russian cause.[78]

At the end of June 2023, Putin's own position looked vulnerable for the first time. Yevgeny Prigozhin, the head of the Wagner Group, had been running a campaign to get Shoigu, the defence minister, and General Valery Gerasimov, Chief of the General Staff, sacked for incompetence, denying Wagner ammunition when they needed it, and insisting on all private military companies coming under central control. This led to Prigozhin directly challenging official narratives on the origins of the war, denying claims about the pre-war situation in the Donbas and describing the subsequent war as a 'meat-grinder'.[79] This led to a short-lived mutiny which was barely opposed and at one point looked like it would turn into a credible coup event, until an intervention by the president of Belarus, Alyaksandr Lukashenka, led to Prigozhin reversing course but avoiding capture and imprisonment. The key domestic challenge to the official narrative had come from a figure who had been close to Putin and could claim a relatively successful role in fighting the war.

Conclusion

In 2014, approximately 70% of Russians believed that events in Ukraine were being covered truthfully, and without bias, by government-owned channels.[80] However, this is not necessarily a reflection of the power of digital information, because approximately 90% of Russians cite television as their principal media source.[81] Social media provided another avenue for Russia to deny any involvement in Ukraine in 2014 while simultaneously engaging in whataboutery towards the US and NATO.[82] The impact of digital information operations on the crisis at that time was primarily to reinforce pre-existing views.

These trends were replicated in the lead-up to and after the 2022 invasion. According to surveys, 60% of Russians supported the invasion, which may largely be attributed to their reliance on and trusting of the traditional, state-controlled news sources, particularly television: as Kseniya Kizlova and Pippa Norris put it, 'state propaganda on television and censorship of independent social media has isolated the country and successfully brainwashed numerous citizens to obediently repeat the narratives "as heard on TV"'.[83] However, as Russian setbacks in the land battles became impossible to ignore, and then when the mobilisation of reservists announced in September 2022 was implemented chaotically, even the state media struggled to explain what had gone wrong and how the situation could be retrieved.

Addressing Russia's strategy more broadly, Pomerantsev argues that the point of its propaganda 'is not to persuade anyone, but to keep the viewer hooked and distracted – to disrupt Western narratives rather than provide a counternarrative. It is the perfect genre for conspiracy theories, which are all over Russian TV.'[84] In the case of Ukraine, Russia's use of social media amplified television messages to reinforce views among the domestic audience about the merits of Moscow's intervention, but its impact on the crisis itself, or on narratives in other countries, was negligible and even counterproductive.

By contrast, Ukraine's information campaigns, including their digital content, enjoyed notable success in shaping Western narratives about a country being brutally attacked and needing all the help it could get. Ukraine's narrative also had the advantage of fitting far better with the verifiable facts; it was telling its audience something they were prepared to believe. Equally, it was not difficult to persuade the Ukrainian domestic audience of the need to resist, as it was feeling the effects of Russia's aggression at first hand. Ukrainian bloggers had a strong presence on social media, providing up-to-date reports about battlefield developments and posting dramatic videos of Russian units being attacked, often against a background of pop music. As the war dragged on, these increasingly showed death and injury in explicit detail. Others provided translations of Russian posts (often from Telegram) detailing how badly things were going for Russian forces, or the maltreatment of mobilised soldiers. While some of the bloggers did no more than cheerlead, and were prone to optimism that at times became misinformation, a number gained reputations for reliability and attracted large followings. Because Ukrainian operational security was tight, however, they were not quite so informative on Ukrainian losses and setbacks.

Among the pro-Russian bloggers were some who analysed military developments in a way that acknowledged Russian difficulties while emphasising Ukrainian losses and insisting on the inevitability of Russian victory. Many were close to the military but frustrated with the levels of incompetence being demonstrated, and were unsparing in their criticism of the high command – Girkin was an example. There were also many bots that just repeated standard Russian talking points, easily identifiable because they were anonymous and had few followers.

Overall, the Russian information strategy was no more successful than its military strategy. This was despite a doctrinal belief within the Russian security establishment, reinforced by individuals with Federal Security Service (FSB) and Soviet-era Committee for State Security (KGB) backgrounds at its pinnacle, of the importance of psychology and manipulating information to shape perceptions. In his 2015 description of Russia's next-generation warfare, the Israeli analyst Dmitry Adamsky described it as an 'informational-psychological struggle', targeting the adversary's decision-makers and public with the aim of undermining their willingness to use force and ultimately dissuade them from responding to Russia's own actions.[85] When this approach is applied to a situation such as Ukraine, coercion depends on shaping minds *before* events unfold. Democracies were believed to be particularly vulnerable to such efforts, not only because of freedom of speech but also because of the potential to undermine their institutions, taking advantage of the system from within.[86] Based on this logic, digital information campaigns could supposedly convince domestic actors within other states to challenge any policies by their leaders that worked against Russian political interests. If this was indeed what Russian policymakers had believed with regard to the situation in Ukraine, then the war proved them wrong.

CONCLUSION

Our minds are not blank sheets of paper on which outsiders can write what they like. Thoughts are shaped by the milieux in which we live: our inherited cultural traditions, including language; the quality and nature of our education; our interactions with family and friends; and our responses – both emotional and rational – to new events or information.

The digital information environment features new platforms on which a range of actors can operate. Social media has an immediacy and accessibility that other media lack, and it can be designed to appeal to very specific sections of society. It is also noisy and chaotic. As a form of communication it is barely two decades old and is still developing. It was used quite differently, for example, in the 2012, 2016 and 2020 US presidential elections. What happened in the online environment's past may not be a reliable guide to its role in the future. Actors learn from experience, adapt, and innovate. In the 1990s there was much discussion of the impact of TV news channels, described as the 'CNN effect'. This added to the pressure on politicians to respond to events without appropriate reflection and led to concerns that striking images of the horrors of war could lead to pressures to act hastily and perhaps imprudently. There have been instances when an image – a drowned refugee child, for example – could highlight and dramatise an issue, increasing its salience. So it is with social media. There are instances when an item that 'goes viral' can elicit a government response or even cause an international incident. Responses will still depend on how governments view the interests at stake and their available policy options. Social media adds another layer of complexity to the management of crises and the conduct of conflicts, but whether it is transformational is another matter.

The use of social media for disinformation and manipulation by China and Russia has been regularly highlighted. We do not suggest these efforts are anything other than substantial. Nor are they always ineffectual. But we do urge that a sense of perspective should be maintained. These campaigns have limited effects on their own. They are part of wider struggles in which other instruments of power are usually more important. For example, in Russia's efforts to deny that the regime of Bashar al-Assad used chemical weapons against rebels in the Syrian civil war, and to discredit the 'White Helmets' group, what mattered was not so much the disinformation in itself but Russia's institutional advantages as a permanent member of the UN Security Council, which enabled it to undermine and even block international investigations. The same was true of the investigation into the shooting down of MH17. Neither China nor Russia has been able to stop Western news organisations and social-media activists mounting investigations that uncover practices they would prefer to keep secret.

Observers tend not only to underestimate the extent to which Beijing and Moscow fear Western information campaigns but also to overestimate the professionalism with which they wage their own. In 2018, for example, two Russian Military Intelligence Directorate (GRU) officers were unmasked after they had poisoned a former colleague, Sergei Skripal, and his daughter with a nerve agent in Salisbury, England. The Skripals survived but a British woman who later came into contact with the nerve agent was inadvertently killed. The attempts to discredit the evidence again failed, and when the officers' identities were eventually exposed, the Russian responses were risible.[1] The episode not only made Russia's spies look foolish but also highlighted their readiness to murder people on British soil (this was not the first such incident) and led to Western countries expelling spies from Russian embassies.

Digital information campaigns are limited as strategic instruments because of the difficulty of calculating in advance the effects that messages will have, either individually or as a series. Some messages may break through as formal, authoritative statements of a government's position. They are less likely to do so when they depend on anonymous or obscure posts. That is why in Russia's case, for example, the objective is often described as causing confusion or disorientation as a means of subverting elections and public faith in democratic institutions. These are not, however, matters in which Western countries are helpless. Since 2016 there has been far more awareness of the risk of information campaigns and what can be done to expose and thwart them. In response to the potentially detrimental effects of information warfare, disinformation and the manipulation of social media, it is possible to become more resilient and to hold malevolent actors to account. Most importantly, these campaigns depend on existing divisions within the West and diminished confidence in elites and systems of governance. If we were better able to address the sources of division within our societies, there would be fewer opportunities for others to exploit them. Countries such as China, Iran and Russia are opportunists. The best way to combat them, therefore, is to deny them the opportunity to undermine democracy.

Social media was expected to pose a challenge to the ability of authoritarian governments and leaders to control the information and ideas available to their populations. While authoritarian leaders do still fear Western information campaigns, over time this expectation has come to be seen as somewhat utopian. Authoritarian governments have taken steps to limit access to social media and control its content. In doing so they have promoted their own narratives, often with strong nationalist themes; they have used social media as an instrument for deflecting blame and protecting their regimes' images. This was noticeable in how the Chinese government used social media throughout the COVID-19 pandemic, although Beijing was unable to stifle domestic discontent completely.

Our case studies provide no grounds for denying the importance of digital information campaigns, but they do encourage scepticism about their strategic value. Their effects cannot be guaranteed and can take on unintended forms. They are more likely to reinforce strategic success than create it. These campaigns are one aspect of wider political struggles in which other, harder instruments of power are likely to be more important. The most interesting questions revolve around how these campaigns interact with other, more traditional crisis dynamics, including military and economic power. Even the cleverest information campaigns, especially if launched anonymously or from outside the country at which they are targeted, are unlikely to challenge established narratives unless they are supported by real events that require individuals to reappraise what they thought they knew. This is why most narratives during a crisis, which may well be fortified by active messaging, will be targeted at domestic audiences, where they are likely to reinforce existing views. The effects of such campaigns, even when intended for domestic audiences, can be hard to control. Once nationalist fervour has been whipped up it may be difficult to calm it down, which may encourage imprudent escalation. For example, in the US–Iran crisis in January 2020, it is possible to imagine a scenario in which Iran's retaliatory missile strikes killed US military personnel. After Trump's threat to target Iranian cultural sites, would he have followed through on it? Or in March 2019, if Pakistan had refused to return the captured Indian pilot, Modi would have had little choice but to further escalate the crisis, given the upcoming election and the increasingly violent Indian nationalist movement playing out on social media. Furthermore, even successful campaigns may falter if their claims do not match lived experience.

Authoritarian states can build internal echo chambers in an attempt to control the narrative about their own actions. For example, during the Ukraine crisis, the Russian government took advantage of various news agencies that provided an additional platform to spread pro-Russia disinformation. While they typically just repeated official government positions, television news items or stories originating from the Internet Research Agency, they nevertheless had an amplifying effect. The Ukraine case study points to efforts by individuals, groups, organisations and governments to counter Russian disinformation campaigns. With assistance from European actors, the Ukrainian government tracked and shut down bot farms, many of them operating from within Ukraine. Kyiv also blocked access to Russian media and social media on numerous occasions. Meanwhile, investigative groups such as StopFake and Bellingcat have become an essential part of the information ecosystem in challenging fake news and spreading evidence to undermine governments' attempts to distract from or deny the truth.

But social-media companies have been lax about policing disinformation or mitigating the potentially negative impacts of social media. This was especially evident in the India–

Pakistan crisis, when Facebook failed to block the aggressive online harassment of Indian individuals deemed to be insufficiently nationalistic. But it was also evident throughout the COVID-19 pandemic, as evidenced by the failure of numerous platforms to stop the spread of disinformation about the origins of the virus and the efficacy of vaccines. Social-media companies face a paradox: if they fail to block certain kinds of content they will be labelled 'irresponsible', as recently occurred with Facebook; but if they do block content they will be criticised for censorship or pandering to certain political movements. For example, shortly after Soleimani's killing, Instagram removed numerous posts and blocked accounts praising him, on the grounds that they would have been a violation of US sanctions. The company was later widely criticised for this, and the posts were restored.[2] This became a major issue with Twitter after Elon Musk took control, as the monitoring of hate speech and misinformation was given lower priority. Coupled with technical issues with the platform, the effect was to discourage users (and, just as importantly, advertisers) and encourage a search for alternatives, which other companies, including Facebook, were keen to provide.[3] It is too early to assess the effect of these upheavals but the result may be greater fragmentation in the digital media space, undermining its value as a form for both benign and malign communications.

Another concern is collusion between authoritarian governments to spread disinformation. Unconfirmed reports that Russia and China agreed in 2021 to cooperate on propaganda campaigns are potentially of concern.[4] This appears to be a relatively new trend, but it was obvious during the pandemic that China, Iran and Russia were spreading similar (sometimes identical) narratives. All three states have a shared interest in undermining Western democracies and their associated institutions. Conspiracy theories about the origins of COVID-19 and about Western vaccines provided an ideal opportunity to work towards that common goal. Russia, for example, appeared more interested in promoting its own vaccine, Sputnik V, using it as part of an information campaign aimed at international audiences, than in vaccinating its own population.[5]

At the heart of this whole issue is the question of trust. Authoritarian governments put trust at risk when they push narratives increasingly removed from lived reality through state-sponsored echo chambers. If economic growth falters, healthcare systems struggle and military battles are lost, attempts to deny the obvious and paper over the cracks using official propaganda will ultimately fail to prevent support from leaking away. As can be seen with China, once the government is unable to tolerate any dissent or criticism, this leads to increasingly expansive control of what is being said not only in China itself but also around the world, so that disputes over narratives (for example the state of human rights in China) can add new sources of tension. This drives much of the Chinese social-media activity initiated by Beijing. Refusing to permit any challenge to the system, it sets out to control the narratives within its international environment to an extent that is impossible to achieve. There is only so much reality that can be denied.

The situation in the West is different. On the major issues facing government there is no shortage of distinct perspectives, and disagreement is constant. The information environment, created by a mixture of traditional and social media, cannot be controlled and can only be regulated with difficulty. It would be naive to suggest this always keeps the public accurately informed or that the system cannot become subject to serious distortions as a result of ownership issues surrounding major outlets and platforms – but there is a flexibility, both in holding governments to account and in addressing major areas of concern, that more closed systems lack. In the 'narrative wars' of the past, when liberal systems were tested against illiberal ones, Western outlets gained trust when they encouraged candid and self-critical news reporting, just as their illiberal counterparts lost trust because they stuck rigidly to a party line.

We earlier discussed what we termed 'formal' narratives, and the messages intended to reinforce them, which convey the agreed views of organisations, including governments. These have always been the business of diplomacy. Formal statements by government bodies are regularly disseminated on social media but they are unlikely to be much different in construction and content from those that were, and still are, disseminated in official documents and broadcast statements. The concern about Twitter diplomacy aggravating a crisis may have largely been a Donald Trump phenomenon. The issue was not that a tweet could attract attention but that Trump tweeted impetuously and without consultation. It was a function of the character of the man rather than the medium.

By contrast, what we described as 'issue' narratives tend to be highly contested on social media as individuals, groups and governments seek to frame the debates and insert information to promote their own narratives and undermine others. These debates will not be taking place away from other media, whether print or broadcast, but Twitter and other platforms are places where a number of viewpoints can come together and engage or clash. This is an environment where misinformation and manipulation might be rife, and therefore also where governments and those anxious to ensure accuracy and integrity, or just keen to promote their own perspectives, need to be alert and active. The most dangerous narratives for states are those that threaten to deny their legitimacy, for example by exposing corruption or illegitimate uses of power, or by circulating conspiracy theories with a subversive intent. It is their desire to thwart the propagation of narratives challenging their legitimacy that has led authoritarian regimes to attempt to control the internet and even, at times, to shut it down entirely. Democratic governments are expected to be able to absorb hostile commentaries without repression, on the assumption that in the end their fate will be decided through a free election.

The digital information environment is complex and confusing. It has a dark side that will always be difficult to eradicate. There will be consumers of conspiracy theories, online gambling and pornography. Fake news, in some cases spread by fake personalities, will continue to exist. Governments should expect that even if damaging online narratives supporting the policies of hostile powers have little basis in reality, they will sometimes take hold. New technologies enabled by artificial intelligence, such as 'deepfakes' and large language models, may make disinformation easier to produce and harder to identify.[6] Despite these existing and emerging risks, we believe that using information campaigns to change established views in areas of public concern requires – and will still require – significant effort.

An appreciation of the benefits that the digital information environment brings for news, entertainment and social connection should be balanced by an understanding of the risks it brings of exacerbating fake news, personal attacks and demagogic politics, as well as possible ways to mitigate these developments. Our view, however, is that the record so far suggests digital information campaigns will often struggle to overcome basic problems of credibility, even when they are artfully designed, and that they are unlikely to have decisive or escalatory effects on a crisis, or to be more influential than the classical instruments of military and economic power.

.

Introduction

1 Elisa Shearer, 'More Than Eight-in-ten Americans Get News from Digital Devices', Pew Research Center, 12 January 2021, https://www.pewresearch.org/fact-tank/2021/01/12/more-than-eight-in-ten-americans-get-news-from-digital-devices/.

2 Marshall McLuhan, *Understanding Media: The Extensions of Man* (New York: McGraw-Hill, 1964).

3 Purva Grover, Arpan Kumar Kar and Yogesh Dwivedi, 'The Evolution of Social Media Influence – A Literature Review and Research Agenda', *International Journal of Information Management Data Insights*, vol. 2, no. 2, November 2022, https://doi.org/10.1016/j.jjimei.2022.100116.

4 Constance Duncombe, 'The Politics of Twitter: Emotions and the Power of Social Media', *International Political Sociology*, vol. 13, no. 4, 13 August 2019, pp. 409–29, https://doi.org/10.1093/ips/olz013.

5 See, for example, Peter W. Singer and Emerson T. Brooking, 'What Clausewitz Can Teach Us About War on Social Media', *Foreign Affairs*, 4 October 2018, https://www.foreignaffairs.com/articles/2018-10-04/what-clausewitz-can-teach-us-about-war-social-media.

6 Twitter, 'Permanent Suspension of @realDonaldTrump', 8 January 2021, https://blog.twitter.com/en_us/topics/company/2020/suspension.

7 This figure includes retweets. Tweets sent during Trump's presidency are available in the Trump Twitter Archive: https://www.thetrumparchive.com. He averaged 5.7 tweets per day during the first six months in office but this increased to 34.8 per day during the second half of 2020. Niall McCarthy, 'Chart: While He Still Could, How Much Did Donald Trump Tweet?', The Wire, 12 January 2021, https://thewire.in/world/donald-trump-twitter-chart.

8   Donald Trump (@realDonadTrump), tweet, 2 January 2017, https://www.thetrumparchive.com/.

9   Donald Trump (@realDonalTrump), tweet, 3 July 2017. The subsequent tweet reads '...and Japan will put up with this much longer. Perhaps China will put a heavy move on North Korea and end this nonsense once and for all!', 3 July 2017, https://www.thetrumparchive.com/.

10 See, for example, Peter Baker and Choe Sang-Hun, 'Trump Threatens "Fire and Fury" Against North Korea if It Endangers U.S.', *New York Times*, 8 August 2017, https://www.nytimes.com/2017/08/08/world/asia/north-korea-un-sanctions-nuclear-missile-united-nations.html.

11 See, for example, Anna Fifield, 'Kim Jong Un Calls Trump a "Mentally Deranged Dotard"', *Washington Post*, 21 September 2017, https://www.washingtonpost.com/news/worldviews/wp/2017/09/21/north-korean-leader-to-trump-i-will-surely-and-definitely-tame-the-mentally-deranged-u-s-dotard-with-fire/.

12 Bob Woodward, *Fear: Trump in the White House* (New York: Simon and Schuster, 2018), p. 300.

13 Trump was probably referring to numerous recent failed missile tests by North Korea (18 out of 86). Donald Trump (@realDonaldTrump), tweet, 2 January 2018, https://www.thetrumparchive.com.

14 Woodward, *Fear: Trump in the White House*, p. 302.

15 Jeffrey Lewis, *The 2020 Commission Report on the North Korean Nuclear Attacks Against the United States: A Speculative Novel* (Boston, MA: Mariner Books, 2018).

16 Chrystia Freeland (@cafreeland), tweet, 2 August 2018, https://twitter.com/cafreeland/status/1025030172624515072?lang=en.

17 Andrew England and Simon Kerr, 'Saudi Arabia's Furious Attack on Canada Shocks Western Allies', *Financial Times*, 7 August 2018, https://www.ft.com/content/688805d0-9a55-11e8-9702-5946bae86e6d?.

18 Amy Mitchell, Elisa Shearer and Galen Stocking, 'News on Twitter: Consumed by Most Users and Trusted by Many', Pew Research Center's Journalism Project, 15 November 2022, https://www.pewresearch.org/journalism/2021/11/15/news-on-twitter-consumed-by-most-users-and-trusted-by-many.

19 'Number of smartphone mobile network subscriptions worldwide from 2016 to 2022, with forecasts from 2023 to 2028', Statista, 30 March 2023, https://www.statista.com/statistics/330695/number-of-smartphone-users-worldwide; and 'Twitter Users, Stats, Data, and Trends', Datareportal, updated 11 May 2023, https://datareportal.com/essential-twitter-stats.

20 *Ibid.*

21 'Number of monthly active Facebook users worldwide as of 1st quarter 2023', Statista, 9 May 2023, https://www.statista.com/statistics/264810/number-of-monthly-active-facebook-users-worldwide.

22 'Social Media and News Fact Sheet', Pew Research Center, 20 September 2022, https://www.pewresearch.org/journalism/fact-sheet/social-media-and-news-fact-sheet.

23 Vipin Narang and Heather Williams, 'Thermonuclear Twitter?', in Vipin Narang and Scott Sagan (eds), *The*

Fragile Balance of Terror (Ithaca, NY: Cornell University Press, 2023), pp. 63–89.

24 'Understanding Facebook's Fact-checking Program', Meta, November 2019, https://www.facebook.com/gpa/blog/misinformation-resources#:~:text=Facebook%20started%20its%20fact%2Dchecking,40%20languages%20around%20the%20world.

25 Cristiano Lima, 'A Whistleblower's Power: Key Takeaways from the Facebook Papers', *Washington Post*, 26 October 2021, https://www.washingtonpost.com/technology/2021/10/25/what-are-the-facebook-papers/.

26 Sally Adee, 'How Can Facebook and Its Users Burst the "Filter Bubble"?', *New Scientist*, 18 November 2016, https://www.newscientist.com/article/2113246-how-can-facebook-and-its-users-burst-the-filter-bubble/.

27 Jeff Horwitz, 'Facebook Says Its Rules Apply to All. Company Documents Reveal a Secret Elite That's Exempt', *Wall Street Journal*, 13 September 2021, https://www.wsj.com/articles/facebook-files-xcheck-zuckerberg-elite-rules-11631541353?mod=article_inline. See also Jeff Horwitz, 'The Facebook Files: A Wall Street Journal Investigation', *Wall Street Journal*, https://www.wsj.com/articles/the-facebook-files-11631713039.

28 *Ibid.*

29 Dan Milmo, 'Rohingya Sue Facebook for £150bn over Myanmar Genocide', *Guardian*, 6 December 2021, https://www.theguardian.com/technology/2021/dec/06/rohingya-sue-facebook-myanmar-genocide-us-uk-legal-action-social-media-violence.

30 UK Cabinet Office, 'Global Britain in a Competitive Age: The Integrated Review of Security, Defence, Development and Foreign Policy', 2 July 2021, https://www.gov.uk/government/publications/global-britain-in-a-competitive-age-the-integrated-review-of-security-defence-development-and-foreign-policy/global-britain-in-a-competitive-age-the-integrated-review-of-security-defence-development-and-foreign-policy.

31 Margaret S. Marangione, 'Words as Weapons: The 21st Century Information War', *Global Security and Intelligence Studies*, vol. 6, no. 1, Spring/Summer 2021, p. 149, https://gsis.scholasticahq.com/article/25512-words-as-weapons-the-21st-century-information-war.

32 Rebecca Hersman et al., 'Influence and Escalation: Implications of Russian and Chinese Influence Operations for Crisis Management', Center for Strategic and International Studies, 9 November 2021, https://www.csis.org/analysis/influence-and-escalation-implications-russian-and-chinese-influence-operations-crisis.

33 UK Cabinet Office, 'Integrated Review Refresh 2023: Responding to a More Contested and Volatile World', 13 March 2023, https://www.gov.uk/government/publications/integrated-review-refresh-2023-responding-to-a-more-contested-and-volatile-world.

34 See, for example, Peter W. Singer and Emerson T. Brooking, *Like War: The Weaponization of Social Media* (Boston, MA: Houghton Mifflin Harcourt, 2018).

Chapter One

1   Peter W. Singer and Emerson T. Brooking, *Like War: The Weaponization of Social Media* (Boston, MA: Houghton Mifflin Harcourt, 2018).

2   For more on such categorisations, including an argument that 'cognitive' effects are often the most significant consequences of cyber operations, see a forthcoming book in the *Adelphi* series, Marcus Willett's *On Cyber Operations and the Responsible Use of Cyber Power*, due to be published in 2024.

3   Peter W. Singer and Emerson T. Brooking, 'What Clausewitz Can Teach Us About War on Social Media', *Foreign Affairs*, 4 October 2018, https://www.foreignaffairs.com/articles/2018-10-04/what-clausewitz-can-teach-us-about-war-social-media.

4   *Ibid.*

5   Seth Jones, *Three Dangerous Men: Russia, China, Iran and the Rise of Irregular Warfare* (New York: W. W. Norton, 2021).

6   'China Has Lifted a 3-year Ban on Canadian Canola, Ottawa Says', CBC, 18 May 2022, https://www.cbc.ca/news/politics/china-canada-canola-ban-ends-1.6458746; and 'H&M: Fashion Giant Sees China Sales Slump After Xinjiang Boycott', BBC News, 2 July 2021, https://www.bbc.co.uk/news/business-57691415.

7   This is discussed in Lawrence Freedman, *Strategy: A History* (New York: Oxford University Press, 2013), especially chapter 38.

8   See, for example, David Patrikarakos, *War in 140 Characters* (New York: Basic Books, 2017).

9   Shampa Biswas, *Nuclear Desire: Power and the Postcolonial Nuclear Order* (Minneapolis, MN: University of Minnesota Press, 2014), https://www.upress.umn.edu/book-division/books/nuclear-desire.

10 Patrikarakos, *War in 140 Characters*, p. 257.

11 Thomas Zeitzoff, 'How Social Media Is Changing Conflict', *Journal of Conflict Resolution*, vol. 61, no. 9, October 2017, pp. 1978–80, https://doi.org/10.1177/0022002717721392.

12 Singer and Brooking, *Like War: The Weaponization of Social Media*, p. 64.

13 Sarah E. Kreps, *Social Media and International Relations* (Cambridge: Cambridge University Press, 2020); and Jen Schradie, *The Revolution That Wasn't* (Cambridge, MA: Harvard University Press, 2019).

14 Singer and Brooking, 'What Clausewitz Can Teach Us About War on Social Media'.

15 Linus Hagstrom and Karl Gustafsson, 'Narrative Power: How Storytelling Shapes East Asian International Politics', *Cambridge Review of International Affairs*, vol. 32, no. 4, June 2019, pp. 387–406, https://www.tandfonline.com/doi/full/10.1080/09557571.2019.1623498; and Christian Reus-Smit, 'Power, Legitimacy, and Order', *Chinese Journal of International Politics*, vol. 7, no. 3, Autumn 2014, pp. 341–59, https://academic.oup.com/cjip/article-abstract/7/3/341/2863858?redirectedFrom=fulltext.

16 Christopher A. Bail et al., 'Exposure to Opposing Views on Social Media Can Increase Political Polarization', *PNAS*, vol. 115, no. 3711, 28 August 2018, https://www.pnas.org/doi/10.1073/pnas.1804840115.

[17] Lennart Maschmeyer, 'The Subversive Trilemma: Why Cyber Operations Fall Short of Expectations', *International Security*, vol. 46, no. 2, Fall 2021, pp. 51–90.

[18] Carissa Goodwin and Dean Jackson, 'Global Perspectives on Influence Operations Investigations: Shared Challenges, Unequal Resources', Carnegie Endowment for International Peace, 9 February 2022, https://carnegieendowment. org/2022/02/09/global-perspectives- on-influence-operations- investigations-shared-challenges- unequal-resources-pub-86396.

[19] See Glenn Kessler, 'The Hunter Biden Laptop and Claims of "Russian Disinfo"', *Washington Post*, 13 February 2023, https://www.washingtonpost. com/politics/2023/02/13/hunter-biden- laptop-claims-russian-disinfo/; David Folkenflik, 'More Details Emerge in Federal Investigation into Hunter Biden', NPR, 9 April 2022, https:// www.npr.org/2022/04/09/1091859822/ more-details-emerge-in-federal- investigation-into-hunter-biden; and 'Zuckerberg Tells Rogan FBI Warning Prompted Biden Laptop Story Censorship', BBC News, 26 August 2022, https://www.bbc.co.uk/news/ world-us-canada-62688532.

[20] Stephanie Kirchgaessner et al., 'Revealed: The Hacking and Disinformation Team Meddling in Elections', *Guardian*, 15 February 2023, https://www.theguardian. com/world/2023/feb/15/revealed- disinformation-team-jorge-claim- meddling-elections-tal-hanan.

[21] Thomas Rid, *Cyberwar Will Not Take Place* (Oxford: Oxford University Press, 2013).

[22] See, for example, Jeffrey Lewis, 'Bum Dope, Blowback, and the Bomb', in Harold A. Trinkunas, Herbert S. Lin and Benjamin Loehrke (eds), *Three Tweets to Midnight: Effects of the Global Information Ecosystem on the Risk of Nuclear Conflict* (Stanford, CA: Hoover Institution Press, 2020), pp. 159–78. Lewis explores how bad information, including disinformation, can backfire and influence the elites who generate it, warping perceptions and potentially undermining crisis stability.

[23] Che-po Chan and Brian Bridges, 'China, Japan, and the Clash of Nationalisms', *Asian Perspective*, vol. 30, no. 1, 2006, pp. 127–56.

Chapter Two

[1] Vipin Narang and Heather Williams, 'Thermonuclear Twitter?', in Vipin Narang and Scott Sagan (eds), *The Fragile Balance of Terror: Deterrence in the New Nuclear Age* (Ithaca, NY: Cornell University Press, 2022), pp. 63–89, https://www.jstor.org/ stable/10.7591/j.ctv310vm0j. See also Kunal Purohit, 'After Pulwama Terror Attack, WhatsApp Groups Are Fuelling Hypernationalism, Hatred and Warmongering', Firstpost, 16 February 2019, https:// www.firstpost.com/india/after- pulwama-attack-whatsapp-groups- are-fuelling-hypernationalism- hatred-and-war-mongering- 6099461.html.

2   Rifat Fareed, 'Fear Grips Kashmiris Living in India After Deadly Suicide Attack', Al-Jazeera, 16 February 2019, https://www.aljazeera.com/news/2019/2/16/fear-grips-kashmiris-living-in-india-after-deadly-suicide-attack.

3   Cat Zakrzewski et al., 'Facebook Under Fire: How Facebook Neglected the Rest of the World, Fueling Hate Speech and Violence in India', *Washington Post*, 24 October 2021, https://www.washingtonpost.com/technology/2021/10/24/india-facebook-misinformation-hate-speech/.

4   'Kashmir: Why India and Pakistan Fight Over It', BBC News, 8 August 2019, https://www.bbc.com/news/10537286.

5   See, for example, Patricia Lewis et al., 'Too Close for Comfort: Cases of Near Nuclear Use and Options for Policy', Chatham House, 28 April 2014, https://www.chathamhouse.org/2014/04/too-close-comfort-cases-near-nuclear-use-and-options-policy.

6   Ashley J. Tellis, C. Christine Fair and Jamison Jo Medby, *Limited Conflicts Under the Nuclear Umbrella: Indian and Pakistani Lessons from the Kargil Crisis* (Santa Monica, CA: RAND, 2002), https://apps.dtic.mil/sti/pdfs/ADA400858.pdf.

7   See, for example, Benjamin S. Lambeth, 'Airport in India's 1999 Kargil War', *Journal of Strategic Studies*, vol. 35, no. 3, 14 May 2012, pp. 289–316, https://doi.org/10.1080/01402390.2012.665350.

8   Mark S. Bell and Julia Macdonald, 'How Dangerous Was Kargil? Nuclear Crises in Comparative Perspective', *Washington Quarterly*, vol. 42, no. 2, June 2019, pp. 135–48, https://doi.org/10.1080/01636 60X.2019.1626691.

9   Michael Krepon, 'The Stability-Instability Paradox, Misperception, and Escalation Control in South Asia', *Asia Dialogue*, January 2003, p. 2, https://theasiadialogue.com/wp-content/uploads/2017/10/stability-instability-paradox-south-asia.pdf.

10 Sandhya Keelery, 'Social Media Usage in India – Statistics and Facts', Statista, 22 September 2022, https://www.statista.com/topics/5113/social-media-usage-in-india; and Sandhya Keelery, 'Number of Social Media Users Across India as of February 2021, by Platform', Statista, 29 April 2021, https://www.statista.com/statistics/1232311/india-number-of-social-media-users-by-platform.

11 J. Degenhard, 'Forecast of the Number of Facebook Users in India from 2018 to 2027', Statista, 1 June 2021, https://www.statista.com/forecasts/1136430/facebook-users-in-india.

12 Simpon Kemp, 'Digital 2021: Pakistan', Datareportal, 11 February 2021, https://datareportal.com/reports/digital-2021-pakistan.

13 Dan Washburn, 'Interview: How Social Media Helped Imran Khan Dominate Our Year-end Poll', Asia Society, 22 January 2013, https://asiasociety.org/blog/asia/interview-how-social-media-helped-imran-khan-dominate-our-year-end-poll.

14 Omer Farooq Khan, 'Pakistan NSA Blames Indian, Afghan Social Media Accounts for Anti-Pakistan Propaganda', *Times of India*, 12 August 2021, https://timesofindia.indiatimes.com/world/pakistan/pakistan-nsa-blames-indian-afghan-social-media-accounts-for-anti-pakistan-propaganda/articleshow/85254691.cms.

15 Gary Machado Alexandre Alaphilippe, Roman Adamczyk and Antoine Grégoire, 'Indian Chronicles: Deep Dive into a 15-year Operation Targeting the EU and UN to Serve Indian Interests', EU Disinfo Lab, 9 December 2020, https://www.disinfo.eu/publications/indian-chronicles-deep-dive-into-a-15-year-operation-targeting-the-eu-and-un-to-serve-indian-interests.

16 Dipanjan Roy Chaudhury, 'India Calls Out Pakistan for Motivated False Propaganda on Social Media', *Economic Times*, 2 September 2020, https://economictimes.indiatimes.com/tech/internet/india-calls-out-pakistan-for-motivated-false-propaganda-on-social-media/articleshow/77881857.cms?from=mdr; and Riana Pfefferkorn, 'New Intermediary Rules Jeopardize the Security of Indian Internet Users', Stanford University Freeman Spogli Institute for International Studies blog, 3 March 2021, https://fsi.stanford.edu/news/new-intermediary-rules-jeopardize-security-indian-internet-users.

17 Arjun Sidharth, 'Photo of Slain Terrorist Circulated by Indian Media Was Made Using an App', The Wire, 18 February 2019, https://thewire.in/media/photo-of-slain-terrorist-circulated-by-indian-media-is-made-using-an-app.

18 Narendra Modi (@narendramodi), tweet, 14 February 2019, https://twitter.com/narendramodi/status/1096035566670565376.

19 Narendra Modi (@narendramodi), tweet, 16 February 2019, https://twitter.com/narendramodi/status/1096755533070004226.

20 Nitin Gadkari (@nitin_gadkari), tweet, 21 February 2019, https://twitter.com/nitin_gadkari/status/1098567044574916608?lang=en.

21 Ganesh Kumar, 'Pakistan Govt Spokesperson Mohammad Faisal's Personal Twitter Account Suspended', *India Today*, 20 February 2019, https://www.indiatoday.in/world/story/dr-mohammed-faisal-twitter-account-suspended-pakistan-1460292-2019-02-20.

22 'Twitter Suspends Personal Account of Pakistan FO Spokesman over India's Complaints', *Times of India*, 20 February 2019, https://timesofindia.indiatimes.com/world/pakistan/twitter-suspends-personal-account-of-pakistan-fo-spokesman-over-indias-complaints/articleshow/68084550.cms.

23 Subramanian Swamy (@swamy39), tweet, 15 February 2019, https://twitter.com/Swamy39/status/1096250327228170241.

24 'Narendra Modi's Posers on Terrorism Return to Embarrass the Prime Minister', *National Herald*, 17 February 2019, https://www.nationalheraldindia.com/india/narendra-modis-posers-on-terrorism-return-to-embarrass-the-prime-minister.

25 As quoted in 'Kashmir Tensions Rife as Saudi Crown Prince Visits Pakistan, India', France24, 18 February 2019, https://www.france24.com/en/20190218-kashmir-pakistan-india-saudi-crown-prince-mbs-khashoggi-modi.

26 Ankit Panda, 'India Trip Comes amid High Regional Tensions', *Diplomat*, 19 February 2019, https://thediplomat.com/2019/02/saudi-crown-princes-pakistan-india-trips-come-amid-high-regional-tensions/.

Pakistan–Saudi relations would later deteriorate over how to handle Kashmir; in 2020 Pakistan was forced to repay US$1bn of a US$2bn Saudi loan because of the issue. See Adnana Aamir, 'Saudi Arabia Pulls Support for Pakistan as Kashmir Tiff Widens', Nikkei Asia, 10 August 2020, https://asia.nikkei.com/Politics/International-relations/Saudi-Arabia-pulls-support-for-Pakistan-as-Kashmir-tiff-widens.

27 'Pulwama Attack: Guwahati College Professor Receives Threats over FB Post; Suspended by Authorities', National Herald, 17 February 2019, https://www.nationalheraldindia.com/national/pulwama-terror-attack-guwahati-college-professor-receives-threats-over-fb-post-suspended-by-authorities.

28 Joanna Slater, '"I Have Never Felt So Insecure": Kashmiris Face Backlash After Unprecedented Attack', Washington Post, 19 February 2019, https://www.washingtonpost.com/world/asia_pacific/i-have-never-felt-so-insecure-kashmiris-face-backlash-after-unprecedented-attack/2019/02/19/4d0be2e4-3452-11e9-946a-115a5932c45b_story.html. In another incident, four Kashmiri students claimed they had to go into hiding after being suspended from their university and threatened online: Nishita Jha, 'These Women Are Living in Fear After Their College Suspended Them over WhatsApp Message', Buzzfeed, 18 February 2019, https://www.buzzfeednews.com/article/nishitajha/kashmir-attack-whatsapp-students-suspended.

29 Official Account of CRPF (@crpfindia), tweet, 17 February 2019, https://twitter.com/crpfindia/status/1097073158551674881.

30 Mridula Chari et al., 'Clean the Nation: Inside the Facebook Group That Plotted to Get "Anti-nationals" Sacked, Prosecuted', Scroll.in, 19 February 2019, https://scroll.in/article/913666/clean-the-nation-inside-the-facebook-group-plotting-to-get-anti-nationals-sacked-and-prosecuted.

31 'RSS Wing Awards Facebook Group That Targeted "Anti-nationals" Post Pulwama', The Wire, 3 July 2019, https://thewire.in/media/clean-the-nation-facebook-rss-anti-national.

32 Michael Safi, '"WhatsApp Murders": India Struggles to Combat Crimes Linked to Messaging Service', Guardian, 3 July 2018, https://www.theguardian.com/world/2018/jul/03/whatsapp-murders-india-struggles-to-combat-crimes-linked-to-messaging-service.

33 Spokesperson Pakistan Armed Forces (@OfficialDGISPR), tweet, 25 February 2019, https://twitter.com/OfficialDGISPR/status/1100207947022565377?lang=en.

34 Mosharraf Zaidi (@mosharrafzaidi), tweet, 26 February 2019, https://twitter.com/mosharrafzaidi/status/1100229684107898881.

35 Kanchan Gupta (@kanchangupta), tweet, 26 February 2019, https://twitter.com/KanchanGupta/status/1100301307296940032. The Beatles reference could be connected with a song using the melody of 'Let It Be' that featured in a Congress Party video in 2018, calling on Modi to unfollow trolls who were harassing women on social media. See 'Congress Uses Beatles' Iconic Song to Ask PM Modi to Unfollow Trolls', Statesman, 30 June 2018, https://www.thestatesman.com/india/congress-uses-beatles-iconic-

song-to-ask-pm-modi-to-unfollow-trolls-1502655573.html.

36 Narang and Williams, 'Thermonuclear Twitter?'.

37 Jeffrey Lewis, '"Night of Murder": On the Brink of Nuclear War in South Asia', NTI, 6 November 2019, https://www.nti.org/analysis/articles/night-murder-brink-nuclear-war-south-asia/.

38 'India Election Results 2019: Modi Secures Landslide Win', BBC News, 23 May 2019, https://www.bbc.com/news/world-asia-india-48347081.

39 'Social Media Giants Accused of "Silencing" Kashmir Voices', Al-Jazeera, 1 October 2021, https://www.aljazeera.com/news/2021/10/1/kashmir-report-accuses-us-social-media-giants-of-censorship.

40 Philippa Williams and Lipika Kamra, 'India's WhatsApp Election: Political Parties Risk Undermining Democracy with Technology', The Conversation, 28 February 2019, https://theconversation.com/indias-whatsapp-election-political-parties-risk-undermining-democracy-with-technology-111699.

41 Kuma Ultam, 'For PM Modi's 2019 Campaign, BJP Readies Its WhatsApp Plan', Hindustan Times, 29 September 2019, https://www.hindustantimes.com/india-news/bjp-plans-a-whatsapp-campaign-

for-2019-lok-sabha-election/story-lHQBYbxwXHaChc7Akk6hcI.html.

42 Christophe Jaffrelot, 'The BJP's 2019 Election Campaign: Not Business as Usual', *Contemporary South Asia*, vol. 28, no. 2, 2020, pp. 155–77, https://www.tandfonline.com/doi/full/10.1080/09584935.2020.1765985.

43 Dexter Filkins, 'Blood and Soil in Narendra Modi's India', *New Yorker*, 9 December 2019, pp. 1–31.

44 Krepon, 'The Stability-Instability Paradox, Misperception, and Escalation Control in South Asia', p. 13.

45 Jeffrey Lewis, 'Bum Dope, Blowback, and the Bomb: The Effect of Bad Information on Policy-maker Beliefs and Crisis Stability', in Harold A. Trinkunas, Herbert Lin and Benjamin Loehrke (eds), *Three Tweets to Midnight: Effects of the Global Information Ecosystem on the Risk of Nuclear Conflict* (Stanford, CA: Hoover Institution Press, 2020), pp. 159–78. Lewis acknowledges that the 'blowback effect' is a term borrowed from Stephen van Evera, which describes 'the phenomenon by which military propaganda, intended for the public at large, instead influences the views of political leaders'.

46 Jeffrey Michaels, *The Discourse Trap and the US Military: From the War on Terror to the Surge* (London: Palgrave Macmillan, 2013).

Chapter Three

1 Samia Nakhoul, 'U.S. Killing of Iran's Second Most Powerful Man Risks Regional Conflagration', Reuters, 3 January 2020, https://www.reuters.com/article/us-iraq-security-blast-soleimani-

analysi/u-s-killing-of-irans-second-most-powerful-man-risks-regional-conflagration-idUSKBN1Z21TJ.

2 Abbas Milani, 'The Great Satan Myth', *New Republic*, 8 December

2009, https://newrepublic.com/article/71731/the-great-satan-myth.

3   Javad Zarif (@JZarif), tweet, 28 March 2015, https://twitter.com/JZarif/status/581847308167462912.

4   Constance Duncombe, 'Twitter and Transformative Diplomacy: Social Media and Iran–US Relations', *International Affairs*, vol. 93, no. 10, 17 March 2017, pp. 545–62, https://doi.org/10.1093/ia/iix048.

5   Wendy Sherman, *Not for the Faint of Heart: Lessons in Courage, Power and Persistence* (New York: Public Affairs, 2018).

6   To be precise, Trump opted not to continue the sanctions waivers that were part of the agreement.

7   White House Briefing Statement, 'President Donald J. Trump Is Ending United States Participation in an Unacceptable Iran Deal', 8 May 2018, https://trumpwhitehouse.archives.gov/briefings-statements/president-donald-j-trump-ending-united-states-participation-unacceptable-iran-deal/.

8   See, for example, 'Talking Foreign Policy: The U.S.–Iran Crisis', *International Journal of Ethical Leadership*, TFP Radio Broadcast, vol. 7, 20 January 2020, https://scholarlycommons.law.case.edu/ijel/vol7/iss1/12/.

9   Jim Garamone, 'Iran Shoots Down U.S. Global Hawk Operating in International Airspace', US Department of Defense, 20 June 2019, https://www.defense.gov/News/News-Stories/Article/Article/1882497/iran-shoots-down-us-global-hawk-operating-in-international-airspace/.

10 Jonathan Saul and Parisa Hafezi, 'Tehran Fumes as Britain Seizes Iranian Oil Tanker over Syria Sanctions', Reuters, 4 July 2019, https://www.reuters.com/article/us-mideast-iran-tanker/tehran-fumes-as-britain-seizes-iranian-oil-tanker-over-syria-sanctions-idUSKCN1TZ0GN.

11 'Iran Seizes British Tanker in Strait of Hormuz', BBC News, 20 July 2019, https://www.bbc.com/news/uk-49053383.

12 Nasser Karimi and Jon Gambrell, 'Iran Says Missiles Strike Its Oil Tanker Off Saudi Arabia', AP News, 11 October 2019, https://apnews.com/article/donald-trump-middle-east-ap-top-news-iran-saudi-arabia-55f68b50763c40eeb25ee19027573d86.

13 Patrick Kingsley et al., 'Israel's Shadow War with Iran Moves Out to Sea', *New York Times*, 26 March 2021, https://www.nytimes.com/2021/03/26/world/middleeast/israel-iran-shadow-war.html.

14 *Ibid.*

15 Emerson T. Brooking and Suzanne Kianpour, *Iranian Digital Influence Efforts: Guerrilla Broadcasting for the Twenty-first Century* (Washington DC: Atlantic Council, 1 January 2020), p. 10; and 'Special Report: Iran's Leader Ordered Crackdown on Unrest – "Do Whatever It Takes to End It"', Reuters, 23 December 2019, https://www.reuters.com/article/us-iran-protests-specialreport-idUSKBN1YR0QR.

16 Ariane M. Tabatabai, 'Escalation with Iran: Outcomes and Implications for U.S. Interests and Regional Stability', Testimony presented before the House Foreign Affairs Subcommittee on the Middle East, North Africa, and International Terrorism, 28 January 2020, pp. 1–2.

17 Brooking and Kianpour, *Iranian Digital Influence Efforts*, p. 13.

18 *Ibid.*

19 *Ibid.*

20 *Ibid.*

21 *Ibid.*, p. 4.

22 Barbara Starr, 'US Civilian Contractor Killed in Rocket Attack in Iraq', CNN, 27 December 2019, https://edition.cnn.com/2019/12/27/politics/iraq-rocket-attack-contractor-killed/index.html.

23 Donald J. Trump (@realdonaldtrump), tweet, 29 December 2019, https://www.thetrumparchive.com.

24 Lindsey Graham (@LindseyGrahamSC), tweet, 31 December 2019, https://twitter.com/LindseyGrahamSC/status/1212006170732515328?s=20.

25 Imam Sayyid Ali Khamenei (@khamenei_ir), tweet, 1 January 2020, https://twitter.com/khamenei_ir/status/1212307890524053504.

26 Helen Cooper et al., 'As Tensions with Iran Escalated, Trump Opted for Most Extreme Measure', *New York Times*, 4 January 2020, https://www.nytimes.com/2020/01/04/us/politics/trump-suleimani.html.

27 *Ibid.*

28 Maysam Behravesh, 'Soleimani Was More Valuable in Politics', *Foreign Affairs*, January 2020, pp. 1–10.

29 Cooper et al., 'As Tensions with Iran Escalated, Trump Opted for Most Extreme Measure'.

30 Alissa J. Rubin et al., 'Seven Days in January: How Trump Pushed U.S. and Iran to the Brink of War', *New York Times*, 11 January 2020, https://www.nytimes.com/2020/01/11/us/politics/iran-trump.html.

31 Thomas Stephens, 'How "Messenger" Switzerland Deals with the US and Iran', Swissinfo.ch, 7 January 2020, https://www.swissinfo.ch/eng/good-offices_how--messenger--switzerland-deals-with-the-us-and-iran/45474578.

32 Matthew Petti, 'Donald Trump Told Iran Through Switzerland Not to Attack After Suleimani Killing', *National Interest*, 14 January 2020, https://nationalinterest.org/blog/skeptics/donald-trump-told-iran-through-switzerland-not-attack-after-suleimani-killing-164767.

33 Donald J. Trump (@realDonaldTrump), tweet, 3 January 2020, https://twitter.com/realDonaldTrump/status/1213096352072294401?s=20.

34 Javad Zarif (@Jzarif), tweet, 2 January 2020, https://twitter.com/JZarif/status/1212946202280579073.

35 Donald J. Trump (@realDonaldTrump), tweet, 4 January 2020, https://www.thetrumparchive.com.

36 Drew Hinshaw, Joe Parkinson and Benoit Faucon, 'Swiss Back Channel Helped Defuse U.S.–Iran Crisis', *Wall Street Journal*, 10 January 2020, https://www.wsj.com/articles/swiss-back-channel-helped-defuse-u-s-iran-crisis-11578702290.

37 Hugh Hewitt (@hughhewitt), tweet, 5 January 2020, https://twitter.com/hughhewitt/status/1213921905327009792.

38 Mike Pompeo (@SecPompeo), tweet, 7 January 2020, https://twitter.com/SecPompeo/status/1214590219435069443.

39 See, for example, Mike Pompeo (@SecPompeo), tweet, 7 January 2020, https://twitter.com/SecPompeo/status/1214631686819995650.

40 'Omani Minister in Iran Says U.S. Wants to Reduce Tensions – IRNA', Reuters, 7 January 2020, https://www.reuters.com/article/uk-iran-security-iraq-oman-idUKKBN1Z60VZ.

41 Robin Wright, 'Iran Attacks U.S. Forces, Then Both Sides Stand Down', *New Yorker*, 8 January 2020, https://www.newyorker.com/news/our-columnists/iran-attacks-us-forces-then-both-sides-stand-down.

42 Javad Zarif (@JZarif), tweet, 7 January 2020, https://twitter.com/JZarif/status/1214736614217469953.

43 For the English-language version of the post, see Ismaeel Naar and Yaghoub Fazeli, 'Iran's Khamenei Posts Mock Photo Showing Trump "Slap in the Face"', Al Arabiya News, 9 January 2020, https://english.alarabiya.net/media/digital/2020/01/09/Iran-s-Khamenei-posts-mock-photo-showing-Trump-slap-in-the-face-.

44 Donald J. Trump (@realdonaldtrump), tweet, 7 January 2020, https://www.thetrumparchive.com.

45 Rubin et al., 'Seven Days in January: How Trump Pushed U.S. and Iran to the Brink of War'.

46 When the crisis took place, the time difference between Washington and Tehran was eight and a half hours.

47 Javad Zarif (@JZarif), tweet, 10 January 2020, https://twitter.com/search?q=A%20sad%20day.%20Preliminary%20conclusions%20of%20internal%20investigation%20by%20Armed%20Forces&src=typed_query.

48 Ariane Tabatabai, 'How Will Iran React to Another High-profile Assassination?', *Foreign Policy*, 30 November 2020, https://foreignpolicy.com/2020/11/30/how-will-iran-react-to-another-high-profile-assassination/.

49 Ronen Bergman and Farnaz Fassihi, 'The Scientist and the A.I.-assisted, Remote-control Killing Machine', *New York Times*, 18 September 2020, https://www.nytimes.com/2021/09/18/world/middleeast/iran-nuclear-fakhrizadeh-assassination-israel.html?searchResultPosition=1; and Ronna McDaniel (@GOPChairwoman), tweet, 6 January 2020, https://twitter.com/GOPChairwoman/status/1214320404820582400.

50 Elise Labott, 'John Kerry: Some Sanctions Relief Money for Iran Will Go to Terrorism', CNN, 21 January 2016, https://www.cnn.com/2016/01/21/politics/john-kerry-money-iran-sanctions-terrorism/index.html.

51 Lindsey Graham (@LindseyGrahamSC), tweet, 31 December 2019, https://twitter.com/LindseyGrahamSC/status/1212006172628262913; and Marco Rubio (@marcorubio), tweet, 8 January 2020, https://twitter.com/marcorubio/status/1215022043059695616.

52 The Instagram image is no longer available, but it can be seen at 'Tensions Escalate on Social Media Platforms After Soleimani's Death', Medium, 4 January 2020: https://medium.com/dfrlab/tensions-escalate-on-social-media-platforms-after-soleimanis-death-48f295ecec5e.

53 Mark Dubowitz and Saeed Ghasseminejad, 'Iran's COVID-19 Disinformation Campaign', *CTC Sentinel*, vol. 13, no. 6, June 2020, https://www.ctc.usma.edu/irans-covid-19-disinformation-campaign/.

54 Hinshaw, Parkinson and Faucon, 'Swiss Back Channel Helped Defuse U.S.–Iran Crisis'.

Chapter Four

1   'Social Media Use During COVID-19 Worldwide – Statistics & Figures', Statista, 18 October 2022, https://www.statista.com/topics/7863/social-media-use-during-coronavirus-covid-19-worldwide/#:~:text=There%20was%20a%20significant%20increase,stable%20in%20the%20upcoming%20years; and Debra Aho Williamson, 'US Social Media Usage: How the Coronavirus Is Changing Consumer Behavior', Insider Intelligence, 2 June 2020, https://www.emarketer.com/content/us-social-media-usage.

2   Erica Kinetz, 'Anatomy of a Conspiracy: With COVID, China Took Leading Role', Associated Press, 15 February 2021, https://apnews.com/article/pandemics-beijing-only-on-ap-epidemics-media-122b73e134b780919cc1808f3f6f16e8.

3   See Jessica Brandt, 'How Autocrats Manipulate Online Information: Putin's and Xi's Playbooks', *Washington Quarterly*, vol. 44, no. 3, 22 September 2021, pp. 127–54, https://doi.org/10.1080/01636 60X.2021.1970902. According to Brandt, 'Beijing appears to rely on false personas to create the illusion of popular support for its messaging, particularly in circumstances when they are unable to develop substantial, organic traction on their own. That is, where Russia uses false personas to seed polarizing and divisive narratives or to entrap local journalists in an influence campaign, China uses them to make it look like an army of netizens agree with pro-China positions', p. 138.

4   *Ibid*.

5   Scott W. Harold, Nathan Beauchamp-Mustafaga and Jeffrey W. Hornung, 'Chinese Disinformation Efforts on Social Media', RAND Corporation, 2021, https://www.rand.org/pubs/research_reports/RR4373z3.html.

6   *Ibid*.

7   Jon Russell, 'Twitter Estimates That It Has 10 Million Users in China', TechCrunch, 5 July 2016, https://techcrunch.com/2016/07/05/twitter-estimates-that-it-has-10-million-users-in-china/.

8   'Pro-China Posts Spam Taiwan President-elect Tsai's Facebook', BBC News, 21 January 2016, https://www.bbc.com/news/world-asia-china-35368930.

9   Josh Rogin, 'Opinion: China's Interference in the 2018 Elections Succeeded – in Taiwan', *Washington Post*, 18 December 2018, https://www.washingtonpost.com/opinions/2018/12/18/chinas-interference-elections-succeeded-taiwan/.

10 Catherine Cortez Masto et al., Letter to Secretaries Pompeo and Mnuchin and Directors Coats and Wray, 13 December 2018, https://www.washingtonpost.com/r/2010-2019/WashingtonPost/2018/12/18/Editorial-Opinion/Graphics/FINALSenatorCortezMasto TaiwanCCPInterferenceLetter.pdf?itid=lk_inline_manual_5.

11 Atlantic Council, 'China Messaging Across the Strait: China-friendly Narratives and the 2020 Taiwan Presidential Election', December 2020, https://www.atlanticcouncil.org/wp-content/uploads/2020/12/China-Taiwan-FINAL.pdf.

12 Harold, Beauchamp-Mustafaga and Hornung, 'Chinese Disinformation Efforts on Social Media'.

13 Kat Devlin and Christine Huang, 'In Taiwan, Views of Mainland China Mostly Negative', Pew Research Center, 12 May 2020, https://www.pewresearch.org/global/2020/05/12/in-taiwan-views-of-mainland-china-mostly-negative/.

14 Emily Stewart, 'How China Used Facebook, Twitter, and YouTube to Spread Disinformation About the Hong Kong Protests', Vox, 23 August 2019, https://www.vox.com/recode/2019/8/20/20813660/china-facebook-twitter-hong-kong-protests-social-media.

15 Twitter Safety, 'Information Operations Directed at Hong Kong', 19 August 2019, https://blog.twitter.com/en_us/topics/company/2019/information_operations_directed_at_Hong_Kong.

16 Guy Schleffer and Benjamin Miller, 'The Political Effects of Social Media Platforms on Different Regime Types', Texas National Security Review, vol. 4, no. 3, Summer 2021, p. 95, https://tnsr.org/2021/07/the-political-effects-of-social-media-platforms-on-different-regime-types/.

17 Harold, Beauchamp-Mustafaga and Hornung, 'Chinese Disinformation Efforts on Social Media'.

18 Tom Uren, Elise Thomas and Jake Wallis, 'Tweeting Through the Great Firewall', Australian Strategic Policy Institute, 3 September 2019, https://www.aspi.org.au/report/tweeting-through-great-firewall.

19 Brandt, 'How Autocrats Manipulate Online Information: Putin's and Xi's Playbooks'.

20 Schleffer and Miller, 'The Political Effects of Social Media Platforms on Different Regime Types', pp. 86–90.

21 Harold, Beauchamp-Mustafaga and Hornung, 'Chinese Disinformation Efforts on Social Media'.

22 James Pamment, 'The EU's Role in Fighting Disinformation: Taking Back the Initiative', Carnegie Endowment for International Peace, 15 July 2020, https://carnegieendowment.org/2020/07/15/eu-s-role-in-fighting-disinformation-taking-back-initiative-pub-82286. See also Brandt, 'How Autocrats Manipulate Online Information: Putin's and Xi's Playbooks'.

23 Harold, Beauchamp-Mustafaga and Hornung, 'Chinese Disinformation Efforts on Social Media', p. 31.

24 Sarah Cook, 'Beijing Is Getting Better at Disinformation on Global Social Media', Diplomat, 30 March 2021, https://thediplomat.com/2021/03/beijing-is-getting-better-at-disinformation-on-global-social-media/.

25 Brandt, 'How Autocrats Manipulate Online Information: Putin's and Xi's Playbooks', p. 140.

26 The term 'infodemic', first coined by David Rothkopf in 2003, was defined by the WHO as 'an excessive amount of information about a problem, which makes it difficult to identify a solution. They can spread misinformation, disinformation and rumours during a health emergency. Infodemics can hamper an effective public health response and create confusion and distrust among people.' World Health Organization, 'Infodemic', https://www.who.int/health-topics/infodemic#tab=tab_1.

27 Laura Rosenberger and John Garnaut, 'The Interference Operations from Putin's Kremlin and Xi's Communist

Party: Forging a Joint Response', Open Forum, The ASAN Forum, 8 May 2018, https://theasanforum.org/the-interference-operations-from-putins-kremlin-and-xis-communist-party-forging-a-joint-response/.

28 Harold, Beauchamp-Mustafaga and Hornung, 'Chinese Disinformation Efforts on Social Media', p. 19.

29 *Ibid.*, p. 13.

30 Some sources would later claim the government had received reports of the virus as early as November 2019. See, for example, Helen Davidson, 'First Covid-19 Case Happened in November, China Government Records Show – Report', *Guardian*, 13 March 2020, https://www.theguardian.com/world/2020/ `mar/13/first-covid-19-case-happened-in-november-china-government-records-show-report.

31 Tedros Adhanom Ghebreyesus (@DrTedros), tweet, 30 January 2020, https://twitter.com/DrTedros/status/1222982869871669251.

32 Kinetz, 'Anatomy of a Conspiracy: With COVID, China Took Leading Role'.

33 Brandt, 'How Autocrats Manipulate Online Information: Putin's and Xi's Playbooks', p. 136.

34 'Is China Succeeding at Shaping Global Narratives About Covid-19?', Center for Strategic and International Studies, China Power Project, https://chinapower.csis.org/china-covid-disinformation-global-narratives/.

35 *Ibid.*

36 European External Action Service, 'EEAS SPECIAL REPORT UPDATE: Short Assessment of Narratives and Disinformation Around the COVID-19/Coronavirus Pandemic (Updated 2–22 April)', 27 April 2020, p. xii, https://www.eeas.europa.eu/delegations/un-geneva/eeas-special-report-update-short-assessment-narratives-and-disinformation_en.

37 Benjamin Strick, 'Uncovering a Pro-Chinese Government Information Operation on Twitter and Facebook: Analysis of the #MilesGuo Bot Network', Bellingcat, 5 May 2020, https://www.bellingcat.com/news/2020/05/05/uncovering-a-pro-chinese-government-information-operation-on-twitter-and-facebook-analysis-of-the-milesguo-bot-network/.

38 Brandt, 'How Autocrats Manipulate Online Information: Putin's and Xi's Playbooks', p. 142.

39 European External Action Service, 'Short Assessment of Narratives and Disinformation Around the COVID-19/Coronavirus Pandemic' (Update December 2020–April 2021), 20 May 2021, https://euvsdisinfo.eu/eeas-special-report-update-short-assessment-of-narratives-and-disinformation-around-the-covid19-pandemic-updated-23-april-18-may/.

40 Di Francesco Bechis and Gabriele Carrer, 'How China Unleashed Twitter Bots to Spread COVID-19 Propaganda in Italy', Formiche, 31 March 2020. Available at: https://formiche.net/2020/03/china-unleashed-twitter-bots-covid19-propaganda-italy/.

41 Miles Johnson and Yuan Yang, 'Allegations of Doctored Films Fuel Concerns About Beijing Propaganda', *Financial Times*, 3 May 2020, https://www.ft.com/content/ee8ae647-c536-4ec5-bc10-54787b3a265e.

42 Kinetz, 'Anatomy of a Conspiracy: With COVID, China Took Leading Role'.

43 *Ibid.*

44 *Ibid.*

45 Zach Dorfman, 'How Countries Amplify COVID Disinformation', Axios, 17 February 2021, https:// www.axios.com/2021/02/17/ coronavirus-misinformation-china-russia-iran.

46 Edward Wong, Matthew Rosenberg and Julian E. Barnes, 'Chinese Agents Helped Spread Messages That Sowed Virus Panic in U.S., Officials Say', *New York Times*, 22 April 2020, https://www.nytimes. com/2020/04/22/us/politics/ coronavirus-china-disinformation. html?searchResultPosition= 1.

47 *Ibid.*

48 *Ibid.*

49 Andrew Silver and David Cyranoski, 'China Is Tightening Its Grip on Coronavirus Research', *Nature*, 15 April 2020, https://www.nature.com/ articles/d41586-020-01108-y.

50 European External Action Service, 'Short Assessment of Narratives and Disinformation Around the COVID-19/Coronavirus Pandemic', 20 May 2021.

51 European External Action Service, 'Short Assessment of Narratives and Disinformation Around the COVID-19 Pandemic (Update 23 April–18 May)', 20 May 2020, https://euvsdisinfo.eu/eeas-special-report-update-short-assessment-of-narratives-and-disinformation-around-the-covid19-pandemic-updated-23-april-18-may.

52 European External Action Service, 'Short Assessment of Narratives and Disinformation Around the COVID-19/Coronavirus Pandemic', 19 May 2021.

53 Smriti Mallapaty, 'China's COVID Vaccines Have Been Crucial — Now Immunity Is Waning', *Nature*, 14 October 2021, https://www.nature. com/articles/d41586-021-02796-w.

54 International Federation of Journalists, 'The COVID-19 Story: Unmasking China's Global Strategy', 3 June 2021, https://www.ifj.org/ media-centre/news/detail/category/ publications/article/the-covid-19-story-unmasking-chinas-global-strategy.html.

55 Julia Bergin, 'How China Used the Media to Spread Its Covid Narrative – and Win Friends Around the World', Nieman Lab, Harvard University, 14 May 2021, https:// www.niemanlab.org/2021/05/how-china-used-the-media-to-spread-its-covid-narrative-and-win-friends-around-the-world/.

56 *Ibid.*

57 Erik Brattberg et al., 'China's Influence in Southeastern, Central, and Eastern Europe: Vulnerabilities and Resilience in Four Countries', Carnegie Endowment for International Peace, 13 October 2021, https://carnegieendowment. org/2021/10/13/china-s-influence-in-southeastern-central-and-eastern-europe-vulnerabilities-and-resilience-in-four-countries-pub-85415.

58 Richard Q. Turcsányi et al., 'European Public Opinion on China in the Age of COVID-19': Differences and Common Ground Across the Continent', Central European Institute of Asian Studies, 28 March 2021, https://ceias.eu/survey-europeans-views-of-china-in-the-age-of-covid-19/.

59 Cook, 'Beijing Is Getting Better at Disinformation on Global Social Media'.

60 *Ibid.*

61 Pamment, 'The EU's Role in Fighting Disinformation: Taking Back the Initiative'.

62 Daisuke Wakabayashi, 'Chinese Omicron Study Renews Debate over "Zero COVID" Policy', *New York Times*, 21 June 2022, https://www.nytimes.com/2022/06/21/world/asia/china-omicron-study.html.

63 John Liu, 'COVID Defies China's Lockdown, Creating Chaos Ahead of Top Meeting', *New York Times*, 7 October 2022, https://www.nytimes.com/2022/10/07/world/asia/covid-china-lockdowns-chaos.html.

64 Edward White and Qianer Liu, 'China's Disappearing Data Stokes Fears of Hidden Covid Wave', *Financial Times*, 9 December 2022, https://www.ft.com/content/abefb06e-a5a7-432b-85bf-b3250b53836f.

Chapter Five

1 Luke Harding, 'Zelenskiy Open to China's Peace Plan but Rejects Compromise with "Sick" Putin', *Guardian*, 25 February 2023, https://www.theguardian.com/world/2023/feb/24/zelenskiy-open-to-chinas-peace-plan-but-rejects-compromise-with-sick-putin.

2 Jessica Brandt, 'How Autocrats Manipulate Online Information: Putin's and Xi's Playbooks', *Washington Quarterly*, vol. 44, no. 3, 22 September 2021, pp. 127–54, https://doi.org/10.1080/01636 60X.2021.1970902.

3 Guy Schleffer and Benjamin Miller, 'The Political Effects of Social Media Platforms on Different Regime Types', *Texas National Security Review*, vol. 4, no. 3, Summer 2021, p. 86.

4 Olga Onuch, 'EuroMaidan Protests in Ukraine: Social Media Versus Social Networks', *Problems of Post-Communism*, vol. 62, no. 4, 15 June 2015, pp. 217–35, https://doi.org/10.1080/10758216.2015.1037676. See also Miriam Matthews et al., 'Understanding and Defending Against Russia's Malign and Subversive Information Efforts in Europe', RAND Corporation, 2021, https://doi.org/10.7249/rr3160.

5 'Ukraine: Negotiating the News', Human Rights Watch, March 2003, https://www.hrw.org/reports/2003/ukraine0303/Ukraine0303-01.htm.

6 'Leonid Kuchma: Gongadze Murder Case Dropped in Ukraine', BBC News, 14 December 2011, https://www.bbc.com/news/world-europe-16176644.

7 Martin McKee, 'The Poisoning of Victor Yushchenko', *Lancet*, vol. 374, no. 9696, 5 August 2009, https://doi.org/10.1016/S0140-6736(09)61027-8.

8 Brendan Koerner, 'How to Rig a Ukrainian Election', *Slate*, 9 December 2004, https://slate.com/news-and-politics/2004/12/how-to-rig-a-ukrainian-election.html.

9 Steven Lee Myers, 'Ukrainian Court Orders New Vote for Presidency, Citing Fraud', *New York Times*, 4 December 2004, https://www.nytimes.com/2004/12/04/world/europe/ukrainian-court-orders-new-vote-for-presidency-citing-fraud.html.

10 Pavel Polityuk and Richard Balmforth, 'Opposition Demand Recounts in "Stolen" Ukraine Election', Reuters, 5 November 2012, https://www.reuters.com/article/us-ukraine-election-protest/opposition-demand-recounts-in-stolen-ukraine-election-idUSBRE8A40PO20121105.

11 'Ukraine Protests After Yanukovych EU Deal Rejection', BBC News, 3 November 2013, https://www.bbc.com/news/world-europe-25162563.

12 Lawrence Freedman, 'Attrition Before Breakthrough', Comment Is Freed, 8 July 2023, https://samf.substack.com/publish/posts/detail/133683172?referrer=%2Fpublish%2Fposts.

13 P.W. Singer and Emerson T. Brooking, Like War: The Weaponization of Social Media (Boston, MA: Houghton Mifflin Harcourt, 2018), p. 205.

14 Molly McKew, Evidence presented to 'The Scourge of Russian Disinformation: Hearing Before the Commission on Security and Cooperation in Europe', 115th Congress, First Session, 14 September 2017, p. 8.

15 McKew, Evidence presented to 'The Scourge of Russian Disinformation'; James Pamment, 'The EU's Role in Fighting Disinformation: Taking Back the Initiative', Carnegie Endowment for International Peace, 2020; and Cerwyn Moore, 'Russia and Disinformation: The Case of Ukraine', Centre for Research and Evidence on Security Threats, 2019.

16 Brad Roberts, 'On Theories of Victory, Red and Blue', Lawrence Livermore Papers on Global Security no. 7, June 2020, https://cgsr.llnl.gov/content/assets/docs/CGSR-LivermorePaper7.pdf.

17 As quoted in Brian Gruber, 'What Ukraine Wants (Part One)', Medium, 27 February 2022. The original post was at 8pm on 21 November 2013.

18 Serhii Plokhii, 'Goodbye Lenin: A Memory Shift in Revolutionary Ukraine', Ukrainian Research Institute at Harvard University, no date, https://gis.huri.harvard.edu/leninfall.

19 Ulises A. Mejias and Nikolai E. Vokuev, 'Disinformation and the Media: The Case of Russia and Ukraine', Media, Culture and Society, vol. 39, no. 7, October 2017, p. 1035, https://doi.org/10.1177/0163443716686672.

20 Shaun Walker and Oksana Grytsenko, 'Text Messages Warn Ukraine Protesters They Are "Participants in Mass Riot"', Guardian, 21 January 2014, https://www.theguardian.com/world/2014/jan/21/ukraine-unrest-text-messages-protesters-mass-riot.

21 Ellen Nakashima, 'Inside a Russian Disinformation Campaign in Ukraine in 2014', Washington Post, 25 December 2017, https://www.washingtonpost.com/world/national-security/inside-a-russian-disinformation-campaign-in-ukraine-in-2014/2017/12/25/f55b0408-e71d-11e7-ab50-621fe0588340_story.html.

22 Bruce Etling, 'Russia, Ukraine, and the West: Social Media Sentiment in the Euromaidan Protests', Internet Monitor, September 2014, http://nrs.harvard.edu/urn-3:HUL.InstRepos:13031958.

23 Lawrence Freedman, Ukraine and the Art of Strategy (New York: Oxford University Press, 2019), p. 81.

24 Cory Welt, 'Ukraine: Background, Conflict with Russia, and U.S. Policy (R45008)', Congressional Research Service, 19 September 2019.

25 *Ibid*.

26 For more background, see Freedman, *Ukraine and the Art of Strategy*.

27 Moore, 'Russia and Disinformation: The Case of Ukraine', p. 5.

28 Lennart Maschmeyer, 'Digital Disinformation: Evidence from Ukraine', *CSS Analyses in Security Policy*, vol. 278, February 2021, p. 3.

29 Irina Khaldarova and Mervi Pantti, 'Fake News: The Narrative Battle over the Ukrainian Conflict', *Journalism Practice*, vol. 10, no. 7, 2016, pp. 891–901.

30 Mark Galeotti, 'Controlling Chaos: How Russia Manages in Its Political War in Europe', European Council on Foreign Relations, 1 September 2017, https://ecfr.eu/publication/controlling_chaos_how_russia_manages_its_political_war_in_europe/.

31 US Department of State, 'GEC Special Report: Russia's Pillars of Disinformation and Propaganda', August 2020, https://www.state.gov/russias-pillars-of-disinformation-and-propaganda-report/.

32 Todd C. Helmus et al., 'Russian Social Media Influence: Understanding Russian Propaganda in Eastern Europe', RAND Corporation, 2018, p. x, https://www.rand.org/pubs/research_reports/RR2237.html.

33 Yevgeniy Golovchenko, Mareike Hartmann and Rebecca Adler-Nissen, 'State, Media and Civil Society in the Information Warfare over Ukraine: Citizen Curators of Digital Disinformation', *International Affairs*, vol. 94, no. 5, September 2018, p. 976, https://doi.org/10.1093/ia/iiy148.

34 Catherine Dill et al., 'MH17 Anniversary', Arms Control Wonk, 15 July 2016, https://www.armscontrolwonk.com/archive/1201635/mh17-anniversary/. According to the authors, 'Lieutenant-General A.V. Kartapolov, Deputy Chief of the General Staff of the Armed Forces of the Russian Federation, gave a briefing that purportedly implicated Ukrainian military forces in the shoot-down'. The briefing can be viewed at https://www.youtube.com/watch?v=Mz_KNS1nyNk.

35 Eliot Higgins, 'MH17 – The Open Source Evidence', Bellingcat, 8 October 2015, https://www.bellingcat.com/news/uk-and-europe/2015/10/08/mh17-the-open-source-evidence/comment-page-2/; and Bellingcat, 'MH17 – The Open Source Investigation, Three Years Later', 17 July 2017, https://www.bellingcat.com/wp-content/uploads/2017/07/mh17-3rd-anniversary-report.pdf.

36 Singer and Brooking, *Like War: The Weaponization of Social Media*, p. 109.

37 Moore, 'Russia and Disinformation: The Case of Ukraine', p. 7.

38 Peter Pomerantsev, 'Russia and the Menace of Unreality', *Atlantic*, 9 September 2014, pp. 1–23.

39 Alec Luhn, 'MH17: Vast Majority of Russians Believe Ukraine Downed Plane, Poll Finds', *Guardian*, 30 July 2014, https://www.theguardian.com/world/2014/jul/30/mh17-vast-majority-russians-believe-ukraine-downed-plane-poll. See also 'Opinions on the Responsible Party for Shooting Down Malaysia Airlines Flight MH17 in the Netherlands in 2018', Statista, https://www.statista.com/statistics/869526/opinions-on-responsible-party-for-shooting-down-mh17-in-the-netherlands/.

40   See Matthew Luxmore, 'Ahead of MH17 Trial, Russians Appear Skeptical but Open to Its Findings', Radio Free Europe, 8 March 2020, https://www.rferl.org/a/ahead-of-mh17-trial-russians-appear-skeptical-but-open-to-its-findings/30475886.html.

41   Anna Arutunyan, 'How the Kremlin Stumbled on Nationalism', European Council on Foreign Relations, 5 August 2015, https://ecfr.eu/article/commentary_how_the_kremlin_stumbled_on_nationalism3094/.

42   President of Russia, 'Article by Vladimir Putin "On the Historical Unity of Russians and Ukrainians"', 12 July 2021, http://en.kremlin.ru/events/president/news/66181.

43   Glenn Kessler, 'Fact-checking Putin's Speech on Ukraine', *Washington Post*, 23 February 2022, https://www.washingtonpost.com/politics/2022/02/23/fact-checking-putins-speech-ukraine/.

44   Ministry of Foreign Affairs of the Russian Federation, 'Agreement on Measures to Ensure the Security of the Russian Federation and Member States of the North Atlantic Treaty Organization', 17 December 2021, https://mid.ru/ru/foreign_policy/rso/nato/1790803/?lang=en.

45   Khaldarova and Pantti, 'Fake News: The Narrative Battle over the Ukrainian Conflict'.

46   See Stepan Bulbenko, 'Banderovskie fashisty zakhvatyvaiut Ukrainu i beznadezhnyi tsutsvang Yanukovicha' Бандеровские фашисты захватывают Украину и безнадежный цуцванг Януковича [Banderite fascists capture Ukraine and Yanukovych's hopeless Zugzwang], The World and Us, 17 September 2015, http://politobzor.net/show-11626-banderovskie-fashisty-zahvatyvayut-ukrainu-i-beznadezhnyy-cucvang-yanukovicha.html; and Khaldarova and Pantti, 'Fake News: The Narrative Battle over the Ukrainian Conflict'.

47   Nakashima, 'Inside a Russian Disinformation Campaign in Ukraine in 2014'; and Moore, 'Russia and Disinformation: The Case of Ukraine'.

48   Samantha Bradshaw and Philip N. Howard, 'The Global Organization of Social Media Disinformation Campaigns', *Journal of International Affairs*, vol. 71, no. 1.5, 2018, p. 28.

49   RT DE (@de_rt_com), tweet, 6 April 2021, https://twitter.com/de_rt_com/status/1379497418543235072.

50   'Fake Video: How the Pro-Kremlin Media Tried to Accuse Ukraine of Shooting at Migrants', EU vs Disinfo, 30 December 2021, https://euvsdisinfo.eu/fake-video-how-the-pro-kremlin-media-tried-to-accuse-ukraine-of-shooting-at-migrants/.

51   Paul Goode (@jpaulgoode), tweet, 1 March 2022, https://twitter.com/jpaulgoode/status/1498517335203848192?s=20&t=Yp-cemYXgO6S_iSNsaFiOQ; and Vasile Rotaru, '"Mimicking" the West? Russia's Legitimization Discourse from Georgia War to the Annexation of Crimea', *Communist and Post-Communist Studies*, vol. 52, no. 4, December 2019, pp. 311–21, https://doi.org/10.1016/j.postcomstud.2019.10.001.

52   Aton Pustovalov (@djxtrees), tweet, 19 February 2022, https://twitter.com/djxtrees/status/1495193495249772544?s=20&t=KErvrQLrikl3AKD9xNfWPQ.

53 See, for example, David M.
    Herszenhorn, 'Russia Claims US
    Mercenaries Plan Chemical Attack
    in Ukraine', Politico, 21 December
    2022, https://www.politico.eu/article/
    russia-us-mercenaries-plan-chemical-
    attack-ukraine/#:~:text=Russian%20
    Defense%20Minister%20
    Sergei%20Shoigu,region%20
    %E2%80%9Cto%20commit%20
    provocations.%E2%80%9D.

54 John V. Parachini, 'Debunking
    Russian Lies About Biolabs at
    Upcoming UN Meeting', RAND
    Corporation, 12 September 2022,
    https://www.rand.org/blog/2022/09/
    debunking-russian-lies-about-
    biolabs-at-upcoming-un.html#:~:text=
    Additionally%2C%20even%20
    Russian%20sources%20
    have,Russian%20media%20outlets%20
    that%20%E2%80%9Cthe%20'.

55 Paul Kerley and Robert Greenall,
    'Ukraine War: Why Has "Z"
    Become a Russian Pro-war
    Symbol?', BBC News, 7 March
    2022, https://www.bbc.com/news/
    world-europe-60644832.

56 Ministry of Defence of Russia (@
    mil_ru), Instagram post, 31 October
    2022, https://www.instagram.com/p/
    CanFwqyM5m9/.

57 Sebastian Shukla, Alex Marquardt
    and Christian Streib, '"He Said He
    Was Going Towards Kyiv": Russian
    Families Turn to Ukrainian Hotline in
    Desperate Search for Lost Soldiers',
    CNN, 8 March 2022, https://www.
    cnn.com/2022/03/07/europe/ukraine-
    hotline-russian-soldiers-intl-cmd.

58 'Ukraine War: Zelensky Urges
    Russian Troops to Surrender',
    BBC News, 15 March 2022,
    https://www.bbc.com/news/
    world-europe-60748234.

59 Richard Pérez-Peña, 'Refuse to
    Cooperate with the Kremlin's
    War, Zelensky Tells Ukrainians
    and Russians', New York Times, 2
    April 2022, https://www.nytimes.
    com/2022/04/01/world/europe/
    zelensky-russian-military-speech-
    video.html.

60 Isabel van Brugen, Lauren Giella
    and Meghan Roos, 'Ukraine War
    Updates: Zelensky Tells Russians
    to Protest Mobilization', Newsweek,
    22 September 2022, https://www.
    newsweek.com/russia-ukraine-
    protests-news-live-updates-putin-
    mobilization-war-1745303; and
    Jared Gans, 'Zelensky Offers
    Guarantees for Russian Soldiers
    Who Surrender', Hill, 25 September
    2022, https://thehill.com/policy/
    international/3659802-zelensky-
    offers-guarantees-for-russian-
    soldiers-who-surrender.

61 Cat Zakrzewski and Gerrit De
    Vynck, 'The Ukrainian Leader Who
    Is Pushing Silicon Valley to Stand Up
    to Russia', Washington Post, 3 March
    2022, https://www.washingtonpost.
    com/technology/2022/03/02/
    mykhailo-fedorov-ukraine-tech/.

62 Mykhailo Fedorov (@
    FedorovMykhailo), tweet, 26
    February 2022, https://twitter.com/
    FedorovMykhailo/status/1497543633
    293266944?s=20&t=Ef4UoSg7shZ1V
    z0J-Jgxdw.

63 Isobel Koshiw, Lorenzo Tondo
    and Artem Mazhulin, 'Ukraine's
    Southern Offensive "Was Designed
    to Trick Russia"', Guardian, 10
    September 2022, https://www.
    theguardian.com/world/2022/sep/10/
    ukraines-publicised-southern-
    offensive-was-disinformation-
    campaign.

64   US Department of State, 'To Vilify Ukraine, the Kremlin Resorts to Antisemitism', 11 July 2022, https://www.state.gov/disarming-disinformation/to-vilify-ukraine-the-kremlin-resorts-to-antisemitism/.

65   Alastair Smout and Andrew Macaskill, 'Russia May Use Chemical Weapons in False Flag Attack but Not More Broadly, Western Official Says', Reuters, 11 March 2022, https://www.reuters.com/world/russia-may-use-chemical-weapons-false-flag-attack-not-more-broadly-western-2022-03-11.

66   Davey Alba, 'Russia Has Been Laying Groundwork Online for a "False Flag" Operation, Misinformation Researchers Say', *New York Times*, 19 February 2022, https://www.nytimes.com/2022/02/19/business/russia-has-been-laying-groundwork-online-for-a-false-flag-operation-misinformation-researchers-say.html.

67   Colm Quinn, 'Is Ukraine's PR Machine Sputtering?', *Foreign Policy*, 10 August 2022, https://foreignpolicy.com/2022/08/10/ukraine-russia-zelensky-media-social/.

68   Paul McLeary, 'Ukraine in Direct Contact with Musk amid Starlink Drama', Politico, 20 October 2022, https://www.politico.com/news/2022/10/20/ukraine-elon-musk-starlink-00062841.

69   Ministry of Foreign Affairs of the People's Republic of China, 'Foreign Ministry Spokesperson Zhao Lijian's Regular Press Conference on March 8, 2022', https://www.fmprc.gov.cn/mfa_eng/xwfw_665399/s2510_665401/2511_665403/202203/t20220309_10649938.html. It is also noteworthy that, a couple of months after the invasion, certain social-media influencers in China started spreading the pro-Russian narrative that NATO members should convince Ukraine to cede territory and bring the war to an end. See, for example, Weibo influencers such as HeTienEn, UnityByForce and Guyanmuchan.

70   Melissa Hooper, 'The Scourge of Disinformation: Hearing Before the Commission on Security and Cooperation in Europe', Human Rights First, 14 September 2017, https://humanrightsfirst.org/wp-content/uploads/2022/10/Hooper-Helsinki-Testimony-12-Sept.pdf.

71   Maria Snegovaya, 'Putin's Information Warfare in Ukraine: Soviet Origins of Russia's Hybrid Warfare', Russia Report 1, Institute for the Study of War, 1 September 2015, https://www.jstor.org/stable/resrep07921.1.

72   Brandt, 'How Autocrats Manipulate Online Information: Putin's and Xi's Playbooks', p. 134.

73   Freedman, *Ukraine and the Art of Strategy*, p. 137.

74   See Maschmeyer, 'Digital Disinformation: Evidence from Ukraine'.

75   Brandt, 'How Autocrats Manipulate Online Information: Putin's and Xi's Playbooks'.

76   See Moore, 'Russia and Disinformation: The Case of Ukraine'.

77   Pamment, 'The EU's Role in Fighting Disinformation: Taking Back the Initiative', p. 3.

78   Brandt, 'How Autocrats Manipulate Online Information: Putin's and Xi's Playbooks', p. 129.

79   Lawrence Freedman, 'Prigozhin's Mutiny', Comment Is Freed, 24 June 2023, https://samf.substack.com/publish/posts/detail/130568843?referrer=%2Fpublish%2Fposts.

80 Khaldarova and Pantti, 'Fake News: The Narrative Battle over the Ukrainian Conflict'.

81 *Ibid.*

82 See Nick Niedzwiadek, 'Biden Derides Putin's "Ridiculous" Whataboutism', Politico, 16 June 2021, https://www.politico.com/news/2021/06/16/biden-derides-putins-ridiculous-whataboutism-494885. This case was in reference to Putin's attempts to avoid questions about the imprisonment of political dissidents by pointing to the Black Lives Matter movement in the US.

83 Kseniya Kizlova and Pippa Norris, 'What Do Ordinary Russians Really Think About the War in Ukraine?', LSE blog, 17 March 2022, https://blogs.lse.ac.uk/europpblog/2022/03/17/what-do-ordinary-russians-really-think-about-the-war-in-ukraine/.

84 Pomerantsev, 'Russia and the Menace of Unreality'.

85 Dmitry Adamsky, 'Cross-domain Coercion: The Current Russian Art of Strategy', IFRI Proliferation Papers, November 2015, p. 24, https://www.ifri.org/sites/default/files/atoms/files/pp54adamsky.pdf.

86 Heather A. Conley et al., 'The Kremlin Playbook', Center for Strategic and International Studies, 13 October 2016, https://www.csis.org/analysis/kremlin-playbook.

Conclusion

1 'YouGov/Times Polling on Salisbury Poisoning', UK Polling Report, 15 March 2018. Available at: http://ukpollingreport.co.uk/blog/archives/9982.

2 Chris Mills Rodrigo, 'Instagram Takes Heat for Removing Pro-Soleimani Content', *Hill*, 16 January 2020, https://thehill.com/policy/technology/478516-instagram-takes-heat-for-removing-pro-soleimani-content.

3 'The Musk–Zuckerberg Social-media Smackdown', *The Economist*, 8 July 2023, https://www.economist.com/business/2023/07/04/the-musk-zuckerberg-social-media-smackdown.

4 Mara Hvistendahl and Alexey Kovalev, 'Hacked Russian Files Reveal Propaganda Agreement with China', The Intercept, 30 December 2022, https://theintercept.com/2022/12/30/russia-china-news-media-agreement.

5 Vera Michlin-Shapir and Olga Khvostunova, 'The Rise and Fall of Sputnik V', Institute of Modern Russia, October 2021, https://imrussia.org/images/stories/Reports/Sputnik-V/IMR_Sputnik_eng_final_web_v2.pdf.

6 See 'Large Language Models: Fast Proliferation and Budding International Competition', IISS *Strategic Comments*, vol. 29, no. 6, April 2023, https://www.iiss.org/publications/strategic-comments/2023/large-language-models-fast-proliferation-and-budding-international-competition/; Josh Taylor and Alex Hern, '"Godfather of AI" Geoffrey Hinton Quits Google and Warns over Dangers of Misinformation',

Guardian, 2 May 2023, https://www.theguardian.com/technology/2023/may/02/geoffrey-hinton-godfather-of-ai-quits-google-warns-dangers-of-machine-learning; and Adam Satariano and Paul Mozur, 'The People Onscreen Are Fake. The Disinformation Is Real', *New York Times*, 7 February 2023, https://www.nytimes.com/2023/02/07/technology/artificial-intelligence-training-deepfake.html.

INDEX

Six *Adelphi* numbers are published each year by Routledge Journals, an imprint of Taylor & Francis, 4 Park Square, Milton Park, Abingdon, Oxfordshire OX14 4RN, UK.

A subscription to the institution print edition, ISSN 1944-5571, includes free access for any number of concurrent users across a local area network to the online edition, ISSN 1944-558X. Taylor & Francis has a flexible approach to subscriptions enabling us to match individual libraries' requirements. This journal is available via a traditional institutional subscription (either print with free online access, or online-only at a discount) or as part of our libraries, subject collections or archives. For more information on our sales packages please visit www.tandfonline.com/page/librarians.

2023 Annual *Adelphi* Subscription Rates			
Institution	£973	US$1,707	€1,439
Individual	£333	US$571	€457
Online only	£827	US$1,451	€1,223

Dollar rates apply to subscribers outside Europe. Euro rates apply to all subscribers in Europe except the UK and the Republic of Ireland where the pound sterling price applies. All subscriptions are payable in advance and all rates include postage. Journals are sent by air to the USA, Canada, Mexico, India, Japan and Australasia. Subscriptions are entered on an annual basis, i.e., January to December. Payment may be made by sterling cheque, dollar cheque, international money order, National Giro, or credit card (Amex, Visa, Mastercard).

For a complete and up-to-date guide to Taylor & Francis journals and books publishing programmes, and details of advertising in our journals, visit our website: **http://www.tandfonline.com**.

Ordering information:
USA/Canada: Taylor & Francis Inc., Journals Department, 530 Walnut Street, Suite 850, Philadelphia, PA 19106, USA. **UK/Europe/Rest of World:** Routledge Journals, T&F Customer Services, T&F Informa UK Ltd., Sheepen Place, Colchester, Essex, CO3 3LP, UK.

Advertising enquiries to:
USA/Canada: The Advertising Manager, Taylor & Francis Inc., 530 Walnut Street, Suite 850, Philadelphia, PA 19106, USA. Tel: +1 (800) 354 1420. Fax: +1 (215) 207 0050. **UK/Europe/Rest of World**: The Advertising Manager, Routledge Journals, Taylor & Francis, 4 Park Square, Milton Park, Abingdon, Oxfordshire OX14 4RN, UK. Tel: +44 (0) 20 7017 6000. Fax: +44 (0) 20 7017 6336.